Bounce Back Now

Awesome Self Help Tips For Aspiring Entrepreneurs , Startups & Small Business Owners To Bounce Back And Grow In Tough Times

Ravi Kikan

This book is dedicated to all the hustlers in the world.

You might be a student, an aspiring entrepreneur, a growth bound startup, a homemaker, a retired professional or any individual who is thinking or trying to dent our blue planet.

This book is also dedicated to those awesome rockstars who had tried doing something interesting in their lives but fell short of the destination and now are dealing with the fear of failure or depression.

This is your roller coaster, get on this ride.

"Bounce Back Now" is my second book for aspiring entrepreneurs, startups, students, professionals, small business owners & individuals who are thinking about launching or have launched their business despite any tough times and now are planning to move into the future to bounce back and grow.

This book also addresses a very pertinent cause which is also extremely close to my heart ♥

It is my endeavor to support individuals who might be in a closed state of mind, pessimistic, depressed or might have failed in their previous efforts. Having gone through the same time and again, I feel this is a key thing to be addressed. This is like the elephant in the house. The content in this book is all about hope (beyond just business), actionable practical tips and I will try my very best to handhold you as much as I can in this whole book reading journey to bounce back and grow

Remember tough times never last but tough people do.

When you are struggling, the best thing you can do is to reach out to people who can share hope and can guide you in the right direction. Reaching out to people who already have experienced that state of mind or have had multiple experiences in the same domain can give you a great understanding on how unchartered territories would most likely be.

This lays the foundation of a bounce back & growth mindset.

However, No one can guarantee you success in your personal or professional life, I can guarantee that. It is only you as a person who has to always choose what's good for you and what is excellent. You have to finally decide what's your definition of success. Make sure it is realistic at times :)

Everyone might give you their POV (point of view), finally choose the POV that suits you and comes handy. Pick and choose, do that freely, do that often. Finally, It is not about the destination, it is all about that journey that you travel for the destination.

That is life. We start from here

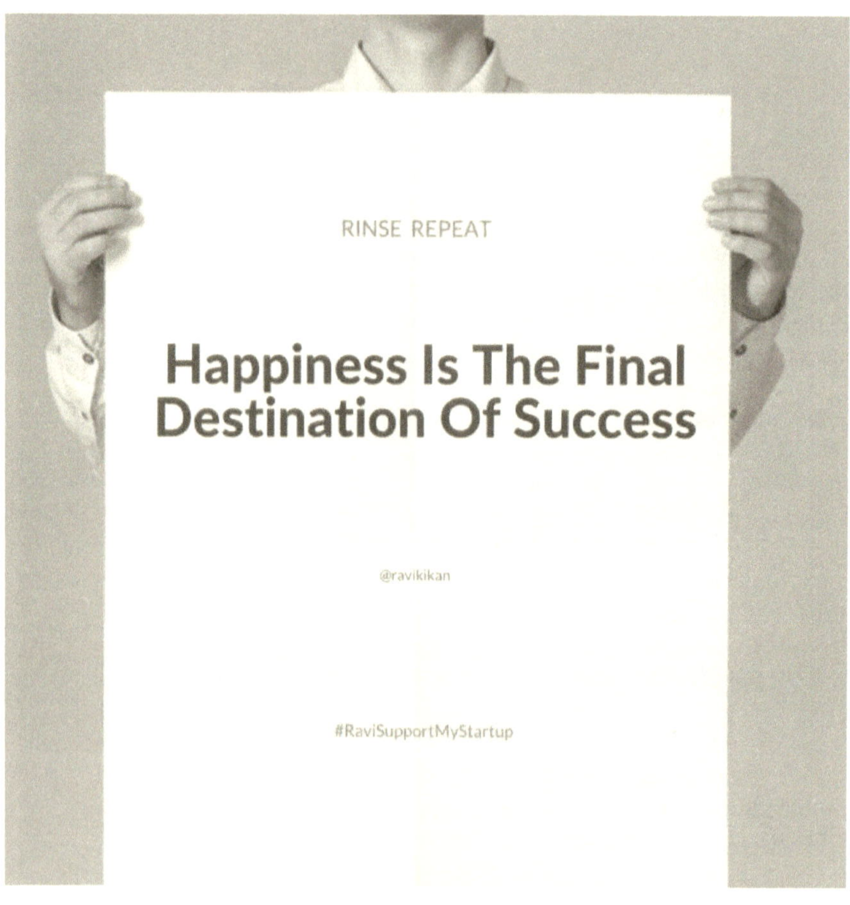
RINSE REPEAT
Happiness Is The Final Destination Of Success
@ravikikan
#RaviSupportMyStartup

What Is Your Definition Of Success ?

Everything is Relative, Keep that in mind.

Before we go ahead and discuss scaling your business, how you can bounce back or how you can build up your business in tough times, here is something that would help you in your journey.

Here is a small story, This story might make some sense to you.

I belong from a very small town in India & have been a kid of 80-90s which is typically Generation X as we would fondly say. My first school was a convent school & let me honestly tell you that I was extremely poor in written & spoken English. In fact I was extremely horrible :)

I clearly remember being flogged for the same reasons many times, for not speaking fluently in English during the school . I used to always wonder whether I would ever speak or write in English fluently. Well that was how I always thought until I changed my first school.

My English teacher in my second school inspired me a lot to unlearn & relearn.

She ensured that my English grammar and diction were improving everyday. Suddenly I found a new love in English, thanks to my English teacher. The only thing that I was fearful of and to me that looked like Mount Everest, eventually became a subject that I loved the most. I am still thankful to my English teacher for handholding me and believing in me.

Years later I wrote a book in English, in fact it was my first book How To Validate Your Startup Business Idea. Of course the point was NOT to just write in English or to prove that I have flair for the subject but to help startups & aspiring entrepreneurs at large in validating their business idea.

I am happy about this when I look back. Small win in my life. A small but a very joyful one. That's exactly my point.

The small little things and wins that bring you happiness are critical things that you should adore and relish in life. These are small pivotal milestones of your life.

These SMALL WINS in your life are also your success pit stops.

Honestly it finally boils down to what brings you happiness in the end. Be it anything, ONLY you choose that.

For me it has been my small wins, you can choose yours :)

Life is
short
DO STUFF THAT MATTERS
#RaviSupportMyStartup

Don't Give Up

Anyone, Anywhere, Anytime.

Let's start from here. Sometimes it just might take some time to bounce back or it might hit your self realization peak but in the whole blind race of your life don't forget to get a little easy on yourself. That's easy Rule no 1, we continue from here.

People don't realize that in the rat race, don't they ?

I won't give you gyan or tell you what is right and what is wrong but here is something that will help you in your journey. Trust me if you read inbetween the lines and understand where I am coming from. Irrespective of tough times like the ongoing pandemic Covid19 which has been testing your patience, business acumen or more so the economy as a whole, the winners will always find a way out to come out of this chaos and make way for greener pastures. You could be one of them. Remember in whatever you have gone through or are going through, whether :

1. Tough Challenging Times & Economic Turmoils
2. Past Business Failures
3. Personal Losses
4. Depression & Unwanted Pressures
5. High Expectations From Everyone
6. Struggling With Your Idea In Tough Times
7. Loss Of Self Confidence
8. Knowing Not What To Do
9. Failing To Grow As A Venture
10. Major Challenges In terms Of Scaling Up Your Business

Just hold your horses, read as much as you can, believe in yourself, reach out to all the well wishers and get on with your life. The only person who can stop you from bouncing back is YOU. Just bounce back. Pass on some positivity and support, it will go a long way.This book is for you and for everyone who feels that the entire load of the world has come down on their shoulders irrespective of who you are and wherever you are from. Just keep in mind & at every step to keep unlearning & relearning.

Good days are numbered so are the bad days.
Tough times don't last, tough people always do.

These are not sayings but valid assumptions to get you going and sail through tough and unforeseen times. This is it. Time to unlearn and relearn and I can promise you one thing that by the end of this book you will be more process oriented, more positive and more charged up to take on this world with all your might.

Let's do it, Let's walk together. Let's bounce back one step at a time.

e-Meet-Ravi Kikan (Author)

That's me, I advise startups for growth and scaling up and most often now I write to share my experiences with the world.

I love working with global entrepreneurs, startups, aspiring small business owners, digital community builders, institutions, investors & SMBs. Have been instrumental in strategising, building and running startup operations in a CXO/Advisory role along with leading cross functional teams across geographies. I run some of the largest startup communities on LinkedIn and also the group owner and moderator for one of the largest groups on LinkedIn:

Startup Specialists is one of the largest moderated groups for startups, aspiring entrepreneurs amid the 2 million+ groups on LinkedIn. Around 400,000 global startups/entrepreneurs discuss & create invaluable content.

I love mentoring startups, incubators and also take lectures in various B schools covering topics on entrepreneurship, growth & marketing. I wrote one of the best loved books for aspiring startups and entrepreneurs - **How To Validate Your Startup Business Idea**. Anyone planning or thinking about starting up a new venture or business should ideally read this book before going all out and launching business.

Bounce Back Now is my compilation of thoughts and experiences on how anyone who is thinking of starting a new startup business or has already started a business in these tough times should be preparing himself or herself for the future & grow with practical tips and suggestions. I also look forward to your feedback and support to spread the good word and help any budding startups or existing startups to look into the future and prepare for it.

Index

My Digital Community Experience

As I shared with you I run some of the largest digital communities for startups and entrepreneurs on LinkedIn. The best part of leading a big digital startup global community is always getting a global perspective on things and issues.

I have time and again participated in some awesome discussions & conversations with entrepreneurs/startups and also reached out to global experts.

These global experts are successful VCs, Entrepreneurs, Angel Investors, Startup Specialists, Advisors or Mentors & Awesome Students who have seen or are seeing the startup ecosystem more closely than others, so taking their opinion and point of view of the subject meant sharing with you (the reader) a global perspective on the topic so that you wouldn't have got it anywhere else but have a regional and global understanding.

The "second biggest thing" that I learnt while handling digital communities is that networking with people from across the world is very important. You tend to learn so many things that otherwise you would not have ever learnt if you were limited to your own geographies. The unlearning and relearning is fast and very often.

The best part of picking up brains from across the world is also to give a heads up to you in terms of the various criticisms, hurdles, challenges, aspects that they have faced or seen in their careers and experiences. These might differ from geography to geography. So the experiences are myriad in nature and bring out most of the aspects that someone might face while starting up his or her own venture especially at the business validation stage.

Last but not the least is the power of unlearning what you have learnt and relearning new things. This means that you should be willing to adapt to new learnings only once you are receptive and willing to learn new ways of doing things by overwriting or adding to your existing line of thinking.

Finally, Be willing to unlearn and relearn :)

Notes That You Should Take

- Learn from the startup community
- Be a part of the startup ecosystem to learn
- Take myriad views from everyone
- Invest on networking more than anything else
- Check experiences of people around you
- Take criticism in the right spirit
- Check all perspectives but do what you think is right :)
- Always be willing to unlearn and relearn

Global Rockstars & Startup Ecosystem

First things first

Let me Thank The Startup Rockstars, Bowing Down To The Startup Ecosystem Around Us. They are the reason to keep the sanctity in perspective.

I have collated my thoughts and experiences from the startups and enterprises that I have worked with. I also take this opportunity to thank some awesome global professionals who have contributed their thoughts in building this book or have shared their POV (point of view) in public platforms to showcase how they have bounced back or grown in all times. This book will be extremely helpful for students, aspiring entrepreneurs, startups, small business owners & growth bound ventures who might be struggling with their thoughts and market conditions in tough times.

I would love to thank the following extraordinary startup GLOBAL ROCKSTARS without whom this book wouldn't have been possible. These are the people who are startup rockstars in their own domain and some of them took out time and shared their point of view on what they feel is right on the subject while the others shared their POV on growth across digital platforms which I have showcased as pointers.

These are the global experts who have been investors, students, entrepreneurs, mentors, startup specialists, coaches who have been there and done that thing time and again.

It is extremely important when you are going down an unknown path that you collect experiences of people who have been on that path or similar paths in life. What that experience gives you is that **immeasurable high** that you might not get from elsewhere else.

A huge thanks to all these awesome global experts, entrepreneurs, founders & professionals who have either contributed or inspired me directly or indirectly to complete this book:

Praval Kant, Tina Zurbi, Neeraj Saini, Prasad Rajappan, Deepak Kikan, **Raghav Belavadi,** Amy Hammond, Dr. Ramchander Chepyala, Shalin Jain, **Dr. Amrinder Kaur,** Nagraj N, Daya Prakash, S. Koushik Debroy, Ashish Singh, **Dr. Satheesh Kumar Reddy Chinnapapagari,** Dr Holger Streetz, Ese-Osarumen H. Efesomwan, Nitten Bhinhhani, Bandinee Pradhan, Utkarsh Chaurasia, **Sha Alibhai,** Srivats Grandhe, Taher Dhanerawala, Tamara Toti, Raj Swaminathan, Nitin Jain, Anil Lakra.

P.s: Always Thank The Ecosystem Around You :)

Why This Book ?

Knowing That Deep Void, The Unseen Road Ahead

"If You Don't Know Where You Are Going, Any Road Will Get You There"

Alice In Wonderland

This has been my all time favourite saying and I use it so often.

Keep in mind during tough & unprecedented times nothing comes as close as taking some tips from experts, aspiring startups and entrepreneurs who have walked the path or are walking the path as we talk.

Irrespective of which sector you are working and what business you are doing or planning to do keep in mind the following things broadly specially from a business build up and scaling POV :

1. As good days are numbered so are the bad days
2. Your team is the best source for bailing you out
3. Validation of your business idea is very important
4. You need to have some paying customers in your kitty
5. Make sure your focus on revenues is equally important as your hold on costs
6. Focus on more organic outreach rather than paid outreach
7. Make sure you gear up and make task lists for your work in progress
8. Set realistic milestones and achieve them on daily/weekly/monthly basis
9. Do not be bogged down by seeing failures

The Unknown Times & Journey Ahead

The whole objective is for you to know the path you are going and what you might expect on that path. Jumping onto an unknown runway where you don't know where it would lead and what you might expect onway might seem adventurous but then it is more of a guessing game. Lot of things are at stake when you start your business so you better be prepared with some questions and answers yourself so that you are well prepared for your business journey.

Not just because your best friend told you to start a great idea or for that matter you saw an existing gap in the market that you wanted to fulfill ...The idea can be great but it still needs some validation before it goes live in the market. If you don't do a fact check you might regret what you could have done to get your business in shape.

You ALWAYS learn from mistakes but don't repeat them.

Yes, I agree. Lot of entrepreneurs & startups, time and again have made this mistake and have learnt from it. Learn from those basics, Learn from the success, failures, mistakes and experiences from people who have been there and done that time and again. It will not only save you time but money, burnout and stress.

Notes That You Should Take
"Reduce Your Chances Of Failure And Increase Your Chances Of Success"

- Don't Forget The Basics
- Don't Overlook Similar Experiences
- Do Take Stable Advises
- Don't Rush Into Getting Things Done Faster
- Don't Get Misguided
- Don't Overlook Readily Available Data
- Don't ONLY Look At Money But Also The Business Process

Who Is This Book For ?

Tough and challenging times like Covid19 have taken everyone by surprise.

During such tough & unforeseen times neither you nor any of the best experts in the world know how things will progress ahead in the near future. The worst affected in these times are then individuals who are either aspiring to launch their business or the ones who have already launched it.

So what next ?

Ask yourself these questions , loud and clear.

1. Should you just bow down to these times ?
2. Should you ask for help ?
3. Should you pivot your business into something new ?
4. Should you believe in yourself more than anything else ?
5. Should you listen to be more resilient ?

The answer to all these questions will be taken up in this book and you will be glad that at the end of the day you might just have a brilliant perspective to go ahead and beat all odds.

However the first question that we need to answer is this. *Beating the fear of failure.*

Remember Falling is not Failing & Failing is Never Final.

This is exactly what you should ideally be reading before you jump all out in the market to start your own business or your startup. This is irrespective of whether you want to start a product or services based business or you are thinking of planning a new business.

This book is also for startups and entrepreneurs who have taken up a lead and launched their business in these tough times like Covid19

Keep in mind whenever there have been tough times in this world whether a great looming recession or a downturn, fantastic businesses bounced back. They are the reason why we look at the silver lining.

Some of the biggest unicorns were born during the 2008 financial crisis like e.g. Uber, Airbnb, Pinterest and Slack to name a few.

It is imperative that you bring in all your efforts to ensure and keep these things in perspective.

Primarily this book would cover two set of audiences:

1. Aspiring Entrepreneurs
2. Existing Entrepreneurs

So, Ideally Who is this book for ?

Lets drill down some details, so that you have a complete understanding.

1. Someone, thinking or planning to start his or her own business
2. Has an idea for business but doesn't know what to do with it
3. Has an idea but is currently not sure how to go forward
4. Fearful to start a business because of the fear of failure
5. Has started the business but is afraid of scaling up
6. Has failed in business in the past and wants to bounce back again
7. Has no clue how to start a business or be self dependent

So irrespective of whether you are a student, a budding entrepreneur, a homemaker, a retired professional, a corporate employee with a great idea or planning to launch a new product/services, a bunch of friends thinking about a possible solution to an existing problem or issue, a startup who has thought about a product or service or entrepreneur who has already started a business, you are at the right place and at the right time.

This is a book for everyone. This book is for you.

"Who Is This Book For?"

- Startups who have failed in their business once or twice
- Small Business owners who want to restart their business
- Anyone who is wanting to jump into entrepreneurship in tough times
- Thinking or planning to start his or her own business finally
- Has an idea for business but doesn't know what to do with it
- Has an idea but is currently not sure how to go forward
- Wanting to validate his or her business idea
- Fearful to start a business because of the fear of failure
- Stuck at the point of building growth
- Students aspiring to be entrepreneurs
- Budding entrepreneurs
- Existing Small Business Owners
- Aspiring startups
- Homemakers
- Professionals
- Corporates wanting to launch new products
- Startups who have launched a new business
- Entrepreneurs who are struggling on what future will hold for them

" Don't Believe Everything You Think, Validate It"
---- Anonymous

" If Your Work Isn't Fun, You Are Not Playing In The Right Team"
---- Frank Sonnenberg

How To Use This Book ?

Learn At Every Step

The entire content in this book is built on the examples and experiences I have had with global experts, entrepreneurs & startup specialists. Entrepreneurs have tasted success and failures and you get to learn a hell of a lot from them. A lot of hard work has gone in building this content so that YOU can reach your success point in whatever you are planning to do.

My own experiences of success and failures have been very helpful in building and asking critical questions that might be relevant for all budding startups and entrepreneurs who are planning to launch their business or have already launched it and looking at bouncing back & growth.

My objective has been simple, to reach out to you and share with you how best you can override in tough times with keeping your basics in mind. The agenda is simple that you jump into the unknown if you really want to but ensure you carry your head with you along with your heart :)

Make sure you keep the things and the right perspective in mind at every step.

You do not need to be an expert to understand things but yes no harm in learning from experts. Here is how I suggest you should enjoy this book and learn from reading it:

- Think about the business which you want to start or have already started
- Keep a diary and pen ready with you
- Write down each key point from every page you read from this book
- Validate with your business at every point along with whatever you have read
- Write down points that you do not understand or want to understand
- Go back and re-read the pointers and try answering those questions
- Do not lose the grip of the business idea that you want to validate
- Keep in mind that you are building a business and not just a product/service

- Ask questions about your current bottlenecks in scaling up
- *UnLearn and ReLearn*

" Start Where You Are, Use What You Have, Do What You Can "
--- Arthur Ashe

" Be Stubborn On Your Vision But Flexible On Details"
---- Jeff Bezos

"Keep Validating Your Idea, Your Business & Your Market "

- Take Notes
- Write Questions
- Ask Questions
- Look for all Answers
- Try Finding Out Solutions
- Unlearn and Relearn
- Take Taking Notes
- Keep Focussed on Your Business Idea/Product

" The Key To Success Is To Start Before You Are Ready"
---- Marie Forleo

" Sometimes The Biggest Step In The Right Direction Ends Up Being The Biggest Step In Your Life"
---- Steve Maraboli

" Winning Means You Are Willing To Go Longer, Work Harder And Give More Than Anyone Else "
---- Vince Lombardi

" People Inspire You or They Drain You, Pick Them Wisely"
---- Hans F Hanson

"The mind is its own place, and in itself can make a heaven of hell, a hell of heaven.."

Building A Growth & Bounce Back Mindset

As I discussed before you might be among any of the following categories:

- Startups who want to scale up during tough times
- Startups/Entrepreneur who have failed in their business once or twice
- Small Business owners who want to restart their business
- Anyone who is wanting to jump into entrepreneurship in tough times
- Thinking or planning to start his or her own business finally
- You have an idea for business but doesn't know what to do with it
- You have an idea but is currently not sure how to go forward
- Aspiring entrepreneurs wanting to validate his or her new business idea
- Fearful to start a business because of the fear of failure
- Budding entrepreneurs
- Students aspiring to be entrepreneurs
- Existing small business owners
- Homemakers or Working from home mothers
- Professionals who are thinking about starting up
- Corporates wanting to launch new products
- Startups who have launched a new business
- Entrepreneurs who are struggling on what future will hold for them

Now since you know which broad category you fit in, let's build your understanding of how you can approach in refining your understanding to bounce back and build a growth mindset. You now just need to focus on two things :

1. Pre Business Validation Mindset
2. Post Business Validation Mindset

We will go through both the mindset in detail and help you sail through on how you can approach your current situation. Of Course the point is to unlearn and relearn.

The **pre business validation mindset** is when you are planning, thinking, rearranging or ideating to launch a new business. This will help you to dig deep and prepare you to enter the market with more stronger validation of business. This will be your bounce back for launch.

The **post business validation mindset** is when you have validated your business idea, checked the addressable market & product market fit, aligned the target audience & paying customers and in the launch phase or have launched your business. Here the focus is on growth, scaling up, innovation, customer experience etc. This will be your bounce back for growth.

Let's understand them in a little detail.

Pre Business Validation Mindset
Validate Your Business Idea First, Anytime & Anywhere

So, Why Should You Validate Your Startup Business Idea ?

Let's Unlearn & Relearn.

“

No Market Demand, Need or Paying Customers Are Some Of The Key Reasons Why Products & Services Shut Down & Startups Fail Globally.

Don't Do This Mistake
Don't Let Anyone Do This Mistake

Focus On Your Business Idea

Part 1 : The 6 Buckets That You Should Know

Let's start from here now. Great if you already have a startup business idea In these times.

This is the first thing.

It is advisable to work with passion on the same startup idea and build a startup business from it.

Ideally your startup business idea should be from any of these 6 buckets :

1. It is currently solving a real world problem
2. It is aiming to bridge an existing gap in the market
3. You plan to build economies of scale
4. You plan to create a new market altogether (disrupt/innovation)
5. There is an actual NEED for your product i.e. There is an addressable market/customers (large) for your product/services
6. Do I have some customers who are willing to pay ?

So write down which among the above is the right bucket for your business idea ? Keep your mind aligned towards it. Your idea becomes extremely strong if it falls in many buckets.

You can choose or brainstorm to build your idea majorly from any of the above categories however keep your mind and heart working in tandem. You need to assess the startup idea from all directions before you really jump into the business. Nothing wrong with that.

The Second Thing.

The second most important thing is that you **CANNOT** afford to jump into a new business till the time you haven't done a realistic fact check on how feasible is the idea for a business. If you haven't done a feasibility study for the business idea you are surely asking for trouble. Time and again entrepreneurs with great ideas have fallen flat as they did not do a last mile check or never went into the details of the feasibility of the business idea.

This is where both hard work and smart work comes into play. This is where most people fail. Take note of this.

This ebook has been made keeping in mind how an average person looks at a startup idea and what all he or she needs to actually prepare to validate that business idea before he or she goes all out in the market with all guns blazing.

" Whatever The Problem, Be Part Of The Solution "
--- Tina Fey

Notes That You Should Take

"Be Realistic, Ideally Your Idea Should Be From Any Of These 6 Buckets or *The Best Case Scenario*, It Falls Into All These 5 Buckets"

1. It is currently solving a real world problem
2. It is aiming to bridge an existing gap in the market
3. You plan to build economies of scale
4. You plan to create a new market altogether (disrupt/innovation)
5. There is an actual NEED for your product i.e. There is an addressable market/customers (large) for your product/services
6. Do I have some customers who are willing to pay ?

" Your Job Isn't To make Money. It's To Find The Problem That Needs Solving"
--- Robert. T. KiyoSaki

" If You Are Not Willing To Learn, No One Can Help You. If You Are Determined To Learn Than No One Can Stop You"
---- Anonymous

" Believe You Can And You're Halfway There "
---- Theodore Roosevelt

Focus On Your Business Idea

Part 2 : Basic Level Definitions

If you are wanting to become a product company or wanting to launch some new services in the market and looking for business idea validation then these definitions would come very handy.

But before we dig deep, we should know the following :

- MVP (Minimum Viable Product)
- Prototype
- Proof Of Concept (POC)

So what is a MVP ?

A MVP (Minimum Viable Product) is a product version which has very basic features for early adopting customers which you can pitch to them and get initial feedback for product enhancement and development. This connotation as I shared earlier is generally used in the software and SaaS companies.

You have to keep in mind that an MVP has to be just a functional early stage product which can be used by the customers which means it can be sold to the customers and is saleable. An MVP doesn't have to be a perfect full product offering.

An MVP also gives an opportunity to you to test your product features, usage with the customers and get a chance to have scope of improvements. This helps you to mitigate the risk of launching a fully functional complete product and incur costs, time and energy if it fails.

The whole purpose of an MVP is to look into the following things :

1. Test the product early in the market
2. Fast Go To Market Launch
3. Faster Learning on the product and market

4. Reduce risk of failure
5. Reduce load on technology
6. Have a scope to improve the product continuously

So what is a Prototype ?

A Prototype is a first version sample or a model release of a product which is built to test a hypothesis or a concept built for a duplicate to be shown. This term is widely used in hardware, electronics, robotics, iOT, design including software programming.
Prototyping is measured for real working systems and used for evaluation for new design processes to be used by users and analysts.

The whole purpose of Prototyping is to look into the following things for a prospective design :

1. A visual prototype is like an engineering drawing for the product which shows the appearance and interface of the product. This is more User Interface focussed.
2. A working Prototype is a complete or near complete functional copy of the product in the final stage.
3. A User Experience Prototype is built keeping in mind the visual and functionality of the product. Combination of the above two technically.

What is POC ?

Proof Of Concept (POC) is a demonstration in practice of the feasibility of an idea in theory or practical to potentially launch it in the market in the right target audience. It gives the probability if a product or service has a scope of acceptability in the customers that it has been designed for. It is a verifying & feasibility check stage.

The whole purpose of a POC is to look into the following things :

1. Verifying the concept or theory
2. Check the feasibility of the product or service launch

3. Is drivin my data which mostly is primary in nature
4. It may not be a complete product or service offering but an initial idea or concept with some basic outlay to support

Notes That You Should Take
"Test Fast,Test Early,Test Right"

- Test The Feasibility Of The Idea
- Test The Feasibility In The Target Audience
- Does Your Target Audience Really Need Your Product/Services ?
- Build a POC and get ratification
- Get Your Market Data
- Build A MVP/ProtoType and Launch

" Sell The Problem You Solve Not The Product "
--- Anonymous

Focus On Your Business Idea

Part 3 : Basic Business Validation Process

We need to dig in a little more to understand these concepts from a user perspective and not just fancy lexicons out of the tech world :)

It's about the growth stage of your startup and not just your product

e.g. When you develop or think of an *'app as a great idea'* you have basically hunted for a gap or a problem fixing solution and the best way what you feel to cover the gap or to solve the problem is building that app and growing it fast, really fast so that you can reach out to the maximum consumers in a shortest span of time and increasing your business reach and growth.

From the above presumption and vision every venture kicks off at the POC stage. It is the same process of validating your assumptions and your complete business model of how you have thought it to be. It can range from a diversified research , data assumptions to more manual interventions like building pre sales funnels, inquiries to demo the scope of your business AKA " **solution to the big gap or problem**"

So what should we call the Version 1.0 of your product ?

In building through this process e.g. for a software or hardware product "a total visual representation of the product which can be shown through wireframes and in a pictorial mode focussing on the UX/UI and still not being functional with some live data will be a prototype version"

This is what I call as the "Simulation Mode"

e.g. in a tech startup, as soon as the User Experience & Design team can build a prototype which can demo the process and stages of the product from end to end without still in the coding stage, you can always bring this on your feedback table with the actual users to correct the shortcuts and products lacunas.

At this stage no code has gone into the product thus the cost of development is saved for optimizing the product as per the Target Audience. So big changes could be made at no extra costs at this prototyping stage itself and the product could be refined over again.

Once this is ready with all corrections, the prototype can be handed over to the development teams with instructions, playbook for the product and the prototype is ready to convert into the MVP (Minimum Viable Product)

Building the MVP/Prototype & Go To Market Planning

A minimum viable product AKA "MVP" is a fully operational, go to market product that has been built for the consumption of the early adopters & stakeholders (AKA consumers) and suffices the market fit and opportunity gap in the optimum way.

This is more conducive for startups that are planning to launch a product.

An alternate definition also could be

"You can say it is a fully operational prototype coded which is live with the stakeholders and actual consumers built in with a constant loop of feedback for improvement to be in a state of continuous beta"

1. Continuous Beta would mean a basic MVP product that is evolving with constant feedback coming from Actual customers and Prospective Customers.
2. Don't wait for a perfect product, bring out your workable product in the market for continuous testing so that it keeps evolving with feedback.
3. Customers should love the functionality and usage of the product, the other things like colors, design, fonts etc could keep evolving (User Interface)
4. Many startups and entrepreneurs spend too much time, human capital, money, energy and permutations to build a perfect product. This not only hampers the Go To Market Planning for the business but also delays the opportunity cost from the market.

5. There is nothing like a perfect product, every product is evolving and comes out with versions constantly.
6. Believe in going lean and fast to launch your product. Don't keep testing the product in your lab or office, Go out and take feedback as much as you can
7. Keep improving, Keep reaching out to more prospective consumers

So now comes the next set of questions :

- **What is your objective in this whole process ?**
- **Who is your right Target Audience ?**
- **Is your Target Audience beyond your consumers ?**
- **How are you pricing your product or services ?**

Validation of your startup business idea has to be with the right targeting, here are some few steps you should take into consideration :

1. You should first understand whom you want to reach and for what purposes for your product or services E.g. If you are trying to build a prototype of a mobile APP than the UI/UX needs to be fixed, so it would be imperative that you first get to understand e.g. how will the customer want to see my app ?, what kind of color schemes would the app have, what kind of basic UX functionalities the product should have, does these functionalities gel with the right TA (Target Audience) ? Keep testing it with various stakeholders and TA.
2. Validate the idea with the right target audience and stakeholders. This means that people who could be your possible customers and early adopters use your product. E.g. If you have an app that will help locate kids around, do take out time to test the MVP or the prototype with parents in your vicinity, known schools, preschools, parents or your friends who have families and who might be willing to experiment and test your product.
3. With this you always have a chance to go back and fill the gaps that your product might need in the market whether the pointers are design related or functionality related either ways it will help your product.

4. This will also help you price the product appropriately for your target audience. They will have the right aptitude to tell you how much they are willing to shell out for the products or services

5. The other stakeholders could be investors, media etc who might want to test the product/service or have a look at the product/service. Reaching out to investors not for funds but only for feedback of your product or services gives you an edge of understanding how an investor might look into your product/service from an overall business validation point of view. This will also test how much validation and growth planning you have done in the market and for your business. They might be very critical of your business but that's fine, it's ok to do learn and improve on your mistakes. Your reaching out to them gives you an edge in terms of being prepared for being investor friendly and PR friendly. You might also get some eyeballs in the media and investment space. That's always an added advantage.

So now comes the next part of the question :
What results are you seeking through this orientation?

The next important element is to understand what validation are you seeking through the product build up process ?

1. **Is this the right product ?** If you are at the POC stage then it is imperative that the concept needs to be validated first with the target audience at large before you go into any next stage. It is also imperative to understand that either there is a need, gap in the market or a totally new disruptive market you are building with your product and your product falls into any of these 3 basic thumb rule categories.

2. **Will this product work fine ?** Once you are through the POC stage and now into the prototyping , wireframing stage of the product your validation ideally should be about the fixing of the UX and UI for the product. The more iterations with the TA and stakeholders that you do at this stage helps you in building a robust product and saves both time, energy and development cost.

3. **How will this product get acceleration & growth ?** Please understand you are doing a business and it is imperative that business building seeks

revenues and sales. Once you are in the MVP stage and later when you go into public beta (full blown product live in TA) you should be doing critical growth tests for your products and tweaks to ensure the acceptability of the product is faster and to a wide mass audience. Your critical job here is to get the multiplier effect for the product. How fast and how many TA get to access my product and pay for.

4. **Who will help you in your growth and acceleration ?** Are you capacitized to handle the growth and acceleration for the product and services ? Do you have the ability and understanding ? Do you have the right human capital who can do it for you ? Are you prepared for this and have you planned the various phases ?

Yes you should have a plan for superlative growth and quickly reaching your Rocket Point. Let's take an understanding of this growth point for a SaaS based company which needs product downloads.

The Tipping Point for Accelerated Product Downloads in a smaller time frame is The Rocket Point. You might want to detail the growhacking sessions once you have launched your product.

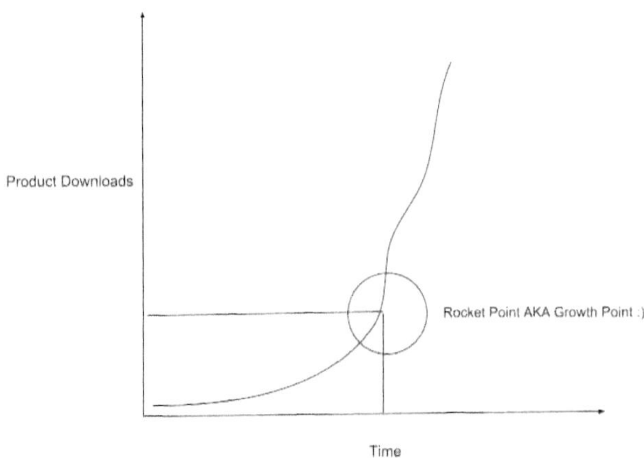

Notes That You Should Take

"Basic Level Business Idea Validation Requires You To Investigate Your Objectives, Target Audience And Launching Your Early Stage Product In The Market"

- Understand Who Are Your Targeting ?
- What Is The Objective Of Your Validation ?
- Understand Product, Market & Growth Parameters
- Getting The POC Done for Validation
- Building Your Prototype/MVP
- Learn About The Product & Take Feedback
- Will The Product Work Fine In The Target Audience ?
- Launching In The Target Audience
- How Are You Planning Growth & Acceleration For Your Product ?
- Who Will Help You In Your Growth ?

Focus On Your Business Idea

Part 4 : The Final Revision

After going through all the details and thoughts on how you need to validate a business idea, here is the synopsis of the whole process which can give you a crux of the whole matter in your business validation process.

Some more useful facts & tips to validate your business idea in a nutshell:

1. **Don't Overlook The Following During Your Business Validation Process:**
   a. Don't overlook the business basics
   b. Don't overlook similar startup experiences in your region and globally
   c. Take stable advice from mentors, advisors, investors, peers
   d. Don't rush into getting things done faster
   e. Don't get misguided with your heart
   f. Don't overlook readily available data in the similar space.
   g. Get some primary or secondary data into perspective to validate the business
   h. Don't ONLY look at money but work on the business process
2. " **Ideally**" your startup business idea should be from any of these 5 buckets :
   a. It is currently solving a real world problem
   b. It is aiming to bridge an existing gap in the market
   c. You plan to build economies of scale
   d. You plan to create a new market altogether (disrupt/innovation)
   e. There is a NEED for your product i.e. There is an addressable market/customers (large) for your product/services
3. **"Prefer" To Work On Your Areas Of Interest or your Hobbies:** or something you might love doing. Time and again people want to do something to follow other people and sometimes they lose interest in the whole process. This ideally this could come out of the following buckets:
   a. Your current hobbies
   b. Things that you would want to do

    c.   Things that you think you are good at

    d.   Things that match with your learnings and education

    e.   Things that inspire you

4. **Insource Your Ability Areas and Outsource Your Weakness Areas** : This means if you are good at tech and coding keep the tech work with you in validation stage and build your POC/MVP however if you need to get some marketing done to either look for a co founder or a team which is good in marketing your products/services. You can always learn and understand things but it takes its own sweet time to do it but it is highly recommended that you outsource critical functions that are not your strength areas or let's say your weak areas. This works great all the time right from the validation stage onwards as you should have your own SWOT Matrix (Strength , Weakness, Opportunities, Threat) ready

5. **Answer these questions Who, Why, When, How, What, Where VERY clearly**

6. Write them down in detail if you want. This will become part of your business plan and/or will clearly help you in answering queries if you are also planning to raise funds. These pointers will also help you crease out a lot of your business validation queries.

    a.   **Who** is my Target Audience (TA) for my product or services ?

        i.   Have I identified and spoken to them or is there a PTP (Promise to pay) for my product/services ?

        ii.   Do I have a ready addressable market ?

        iii.   Do I have some paying customers in my kitty ?

        iv.   Will they agree to pay for my product or services if I approach them ?

        v.   Have I made a list of these prospects ?

        vi.   Have I made a plan to outreach my TA ?

        vii.   What will be my outreach mechanisms ? e.g. Content Marketing, Inbound Marketing , Direct Calling etc

    b.   **Why** would my TA need my product/services ?

        i.   Is there a need/gap/new market/economies of scale ?

        ii.   Is there some primary and secondary validation that I have taken ?

        iii.   Why would the Target Audience buy your product ?

    c.   **When** am I planning to launch and sell ?

i. Have you defined the timelines and worked on it ?

ii. Does it make sense with respect to the Target Audience ?

iii. Is that the right time of the year right to launch ? e.g. You are planning to start a digital marketing company...Generally the budgets of the companies are frozen in March or December so ideally you should start a month or two before this so that you can build your sales pipelines.

d. **How** do you plan to market and sell your product/service ?

  i. How Do you plan to build operations for business ?

  ii. Have you done your homework ?

  iii. How are you planning the various functions of the company

  1. E.g. For your marketing channel , Would you use Direct marketing, Channel marketing, digital marketing etc ?

  2. E.g. For sales are you looking at direct sales or online sales ?

e. **What** are you EXACTLY selling ?

  i. Have you defined your USP (Unique Selling Proposition) ?

  ii. Is there really one USP ? e.g. Are you selling a remedy to an existing problem or are you planning to create a new market altogether ?

  iii. This will define your GTM (Go To Market) Planning before in hand

  iv. What is the kind of pricing ? Have you validated that ?

  v. What is the kind of ROI you are expecting ? e.g. Have you validated with competition ?

  vi. What will be your Burn Rate ? (Monthly operational expenses in total say per month e.g. the total burn rate for my startup is expected to be around 20,000 USD)

  vii. What are the kinds of revenues you are projecting ?

  viii. When are you planning to get the operational breakeven ?

f. **Where** are you selling your products/services? **Where** Will Funds Come From ?

    i. e.g. are you doing it offline, online ? Which is better ?

    ii. Have you worked and iterated on this ?

    iii. Where is your TA located ? Have you validated this ?

    iv. How am I funding my costs ? Where are the funds coming ?

    v. Do I have funds till the time I get **Breakeven** ?

7. Addendum to point no 1 is " **Have valid, relevant and latest data** " with you for building your projections for each of the points mentioned below. This could be both primary and secondary data. Let's take an example of say building a business for ebooks for Abacus.

   E.g. Who is my TA for selling e-books for Abacus ?

   a. Is it for junior section students from class 1 to class 5 ?

   b. Is it teachers who would be teaching those students ?

   c. Is it parents ?

   d. Now when i have identified e.g. this ebook is targeted at all the above, then I need to have some relevant data in terms of **WHERE** I need to sell. So lets say i need to sell this ebook in New Delhi, Mumbai and Singapore.

   e. Then i need to decide **HOW** e.g. Offline or Online or Franchise or Channel partners

   f. How is my competition doing it ?

   g. How is the TA responding to the current demand in the market ?

   h. For all the above if I have some secondary data and some first point primary data I can **MOST LIKELY** validate my business planning.

8. **No Shortcuts To Success** - Take the long way for doing this with no shortcuts. Real evaluation: First, define who would buy what you're thinking of. Then, if B2C or B2B, find a way of meeting them - in-person (conferences, trade shows, cold calling, etc.). If B2C, primary sources are manufacturers, distributors, retailers selling to your prospects, and meet them the same way. Good approach, "I'm thinking about doing such-and-such. What do you think?". And LISTEN. You'll soon know whether the idea is worth pursuing - and if it is, you'll gain a whole new light on what it is you need to pursue.

9. **"Try the Business Model Canvas approach"** which is efficient even if you don't have a business model yet. It helps you, ask the questions.. E.g.
    a. What is my "idea" value proposition ?
    b. Who are my customers ?
    c. How will I engage with them ?
    d. How would I generate money ?
    e. What are the channels I would use ?
    f. Who would be my key partners ?
    g. What will be my key cost and revenue streams ?

You can download a clear version of Business Model Canvas: By Business Model Alchemist - http://www.businessmodelalchemist.com/tools, CC BY-SA 1.0

10. **Build A Product Life Cycle Board (PLCB):** If you are planning to launch a product than this PLCB might be useful to you for the following things :
    a. Building matrix for the idea
    b. How to gather the right and relevant data for your product/market ?
    c. What will be your strategy for product roll out and business case ?
    d. What will be your Go To Market planning ?
    e. How will you build, deploy & test and take feedback from early adopters ?
    f. How to plan your growth ?

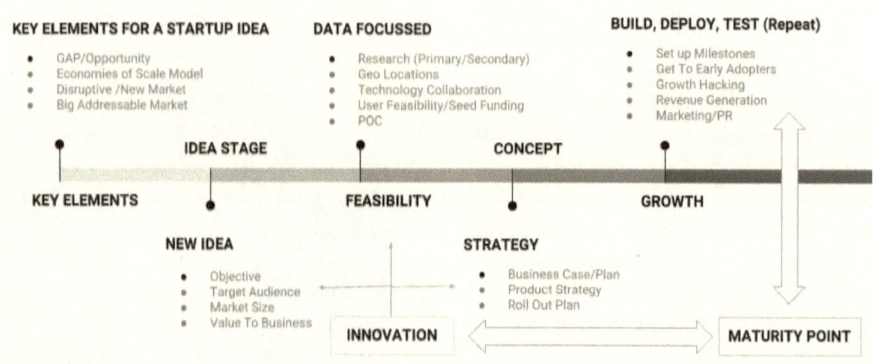

11. **Forget spreadsheets** , if you don't like them , forget BM canvas if you don't like it ! But at the end of the day you need to put figures somewhere, you need some data to bring your idea to the market. Keep your data ready.

12. **When you have your customers working with you,** there's no need for deep evaluation, iterations and structuring. Have your customers test your prototype and give you feedback, time and again to improve your product and services. This is the best shortcut, Go lean, go to your customers first :)

13. **Building a Prototype & MVP (Minimum Viable Product)** and testing with the close knit customers you may have and get the product tested and build it up.

    a. Then you can later reach the markets at large and plan your GTM (Go to market) planning.

    b. How fast you can build your prototype and take it to your customers to test the product is the key.

    c. Once the POC (Proof Of Concept) Is validated you can build your MVP and take it back to the Target Audience/Customers and start refining your product.

d. Go Early, Go Lean, Go Fast, Keep improving. Don't wait for perfection.

14. **Hire a Mentor or Advisor** : It is Priceless to have a mentor/advisor on board from the early stages of the business idea validation.

    a. He or she not only helps you in handholding through the process,
    b. He or she critically looks at the idea and feasibility at all steps with you.
    c. Without looking here and there it is one thing that you should look at from the inception stage itself

15. **Don't EVER Rush** : There is absolutely no need to rush into your business till you have done the groundwork completely. All opportunities and possibilities can wait. The money won't fly away, the business will not fly away. First you need to valid your idea and once you have done that get into your business or go ahead sign some documents.

16. **Trust Diligently** : Do not blindly trust ANYONE before you have done the validation of your business idea completely.

    a. Post that you can go ahead and discuss details with your co founders or your partners.
    b. If you feel otherwise and have rightful questions, go ahead ask them and you need answers for the same.
    c. Do not sit quiet till all your queries whether spoken or unspoken have been answered completely.
    d. Ask questions, it's better to be foolish in the start when you are in the inquisitive stage then be doomed in the end with million questions unanswered

17. **Hiring Teams** : Do not hire any teams or employees till the time you have not validated your business idea and done some due diligence on the business. This is the single biggest mistake that anyone can do, you are basically risking not only business but some careers as well with this. Keep in mind the structuring of the business can be done well and fast once you have validated your business and you have a strong product (Tested in the right Target Audience)

18. **Choosing the right Co-Founder**: Once you have validated your business idea and structured the entire business planning in your head should you discuss the idea of bringing some 'Reliable' co-founder on board if required. You would by now know why and what will a co-founder do in

the business as you have structured the entire business and validated it with your data. You would be clear in your Go To market planning. Having a Co-Founder is not an absolute necessity however:

    a.   If there is a possible synergy for business , you can explore this option and on board one.

    b.   If you do not have the required skills in your validated business model then you should look at like minded people

    c.   Keep ethics and integrity as the top elements to screen

    d.   Prefer having a Co-Founders agreement to avoid any hassles in the future even if you are working with you best friends or family

19. **Human Capital :** This is the most important thing that you should understand at the validation stage. Howsoever powerful or disruptive your business idea might be but if you don't have the right human capital (beyond the co-founders) you are asking for serious trouble. Let me simply for you. Now if you have validated your business idea potential, here is what is important for you to know which of these three you are falling ino:

    a.   A great team with a validated business idea

    b.   A non competent team with a great validated idea

    c.   A great team with a validated idea

You can afford to be in buckets a & c but never in the bucket b. You are asking for trouble if you fall in bucket b.

20. **Legal Documentation**: Do not get into any agreements, documentation or collaboration in a legal format till the time you have done your primary and secondary homework on your business idea validation and you are sure you are going in a certain direction.

    a.   E.g. you want to start a mobile app for parents to locate their kids in the daycare on what they are doing at a certain point of time.

    b.   Don't rush into building legal agreements with schools, vendors etc

    c.   Once you have validated all of the who, where, why, when , how of the business idea then only get on to building a LLP or LLC for your venture or say plan and hire human capital.

    d.   Point c will give you the scope of work and the legal agreements that you might want to work with

e.   Check the requirement for Intellectual Property for your product or services

f.   Consult a lawyer or legal specialist for various things like trademark, IP, patents etc which might be used for your product or services

21. **Talk To Existing Entrepreneurs** : That's the best thing you can invest in. Talking to entrepreneurs, especially the ones who have been on the same road and time and again done the same thing over and over again. They might share their point of view on the following things :

a.   Talk to entrepreneurs Regionally & Globally, you might find different and varied perspectives

b.   Reach out to as many entrepreneurs as you can and do it constantly...Entrepreneurs are busy people, you will eventually also get busy so keep reaching out to them time and again. Ensure you reach out to many entrepreneurs, only few might revert so that's fine but keep the dialogue open and on a larger perspective. Don't give up on this.

c.   Ask them: What to do and What not to do ?

d.   Ask them: How to approach the business ?

e.   Ask them: How to plan for growth ?

f.   Ask them: What kind of costs and revenues you might have ?

g.   Ask them: What kind of challenges you might face in the market ?

h.   Ask them: What kind of human capital you might need for the business ?

i.   Ask them: When should you ideally start your business ?

j.   Ask them: How to build a good startup culture ?

k.   Ask them: How to hire a good team ?

l.   Ask them: How to start your business with what you already have ?

m.   Ask them: How to get data and what kind of data might be required to validate your business idea ?

22. **Ability :** You should for sure know this and answer. If you can't then you should ask your mentor or your advisor to help you out. The question is simple to ask yourself " **Do I have the ability to lead and execute this business that I am about to start ?** " If the answer is Yes from all sides,

it's fair BUT if the answer is a big fat NO then you need to seriously think about it . Do not jump into ANY business whether lucrative or not if :

- a. You do not have the right technical expertise to run the business. This means either you should know about how the business will happen or you should have the right human capital who can help you in building the business. This is because the dependability on the business will be huge on the experts who are required to run the business for you E.g. you want to start a GMAT coaching centre, now either you have cracked the GMAT yourself and you know the whole process OR you have some identified employees who can do it for you who have been doing this time and again OR you have a co-founder who is an expert in this business. Your expert coaches will be the pillars of your business to start with, you should have that clarity from day 1.
- b. If you do not have the technical expertise to run a particular business then you should have the business acumen to run the business and hire the right kind of human capital/co-founder. This drastically reduces the chances of your failure else in such a business , a shift in your human capital can possibly collapse your whole business.

23. **Market Entry Barriers :** e.g. you want to start a digital marketing agency, unless and until you know this business and you know how it operates plus you have some existing customers identified who are willing to pay for your services don't get into this business. The biggest reason is that there are no market barriers for anyone to start this kind of business, it doesn't require a herculean understanding or technical learning/expertise so you might hit into a pricing crunch with respect to a lot of competition in the market from freelancers/agencies etc. So you should do your homework and market feasibility before getting into a generic business which does not have a lot of market entry barriers

24. **Build The Product/Services Roadmap**: Before you actually think about starting your business:
    - a. You should write down the validation process and journey on what are the kind of milestones that you need to achieve or win.
    - b. This would form the preface of your total business plan if you actually jump into the business.

c. These milestones should have strict timelines to follow so that you work with deadlines and know that you have something tangible to achieve. Most of the entrepreneurs miss out on this and miss the bus as they do not have a predefined roadmap to go to and achieve.

25. **Build Your Business Idea Board:** Prepare your business idea board very early in your business idea stage so that during the validation process you can start highlighting the key pointers and revisit them now and then. This will be a perfect revision and validation for you.

26. **Networking : Reach Out To Your Network :** Test the idea and their understanding of the business with your friends, peers, family, whoever you are comfortable in reaching out to. Don't Shy at all, The more people you reach out to , the more perspective will you get for the business idea. As I said before, don't get carried away with critical remarks, those remarks and suggestions might be good for you to rethink your product/services roadmap.

27. **Do You Have Complete Clarity In What You Are Trying To Achieve**: Only once you are clear in your milestones of the validation process should you go ahead. You should have absolute clarity in terms of the following for your business :
    a. What are you planning to do ?
    b. How do you plan to execute it ?
    c. When do you plan to start it ?
    d. Where are you planning to start it ?
    e. Who are your target audience ? Do they want to buy your product/services ?
    f. Is this business financially feasible ?
    g. How is the competition doing it ?

28. **Operational Break Even :** While you are validating your startup business idea you should also keep this in mind that when are you breaking even on the operational expenses. This will help you in streamlining and validating how much funds you might require to run your business and when are you expecting to get into revenue positive stages E.g. The total Operating Expenses for your business might be the following:
    a. Working Capital

b. Fixed Expenses like software, hardware etc
c. Variable Expenses like salaries, incentives electricity etc
d. Overhead Expenses

Now let us assume the Total Operating Expenses is X per month for your business. Let us assume your projected revenue is Y per month.

You will operationally breakeven when Y becomes greater than X.

<u>**Complete Breakeven**</u>: You will attain a complete break even when your revenues will be able to cover the operating costs along with all expenses that have been put into the business including one time costs as well e.g. Infrastructure building costs etc.

- Let us assume the Total Operating Expenses is X per month for your business.
- Let us assume the Total One Time Costs like Infra and Development Costs is B. Let us say we amortize this cost over a period of 12 months so this becomes $B/12 = Z$ per month
- Now your fully loaded costs per month is $B + Z$
- Let us assume your projected revenue is Y per month for your business
- You attain a complete break even when Y is greater than $B + Z$ or $Y - (B + Z) = $ Positive

29. **Stage Of Funds**: Last not least this is super critical to evaluate the following for your business post your validation stage, you should have a defined idea if not the complete evaluation:
    a. How much funds would require to run the venture for at least 18 months?
    b. Do you have enough funds to sustain the first stage-12 months ?
    c. Have you built your cost vs revenue planning ?
    d. Have you planned your next rounds of funds ?
    e. When would you require funds, What stages ?
    f. Have you identified the investors who might be interested ?
    g. Have you built your pitch deck ?
    h. Is Your Go To Market for investors ready ?
    i. Are you an investor ready business yourself ?

" Stay Patient and Trust Your Journey"
---- Anonymous

" Outstanding People Have One Thing In Common : An Absolute Sense Of Mission"
---- Zig Ziglar

Notes That You Should Take

"Final Pointers For Startup Business Validation That You Should Know"

- Don't Overlook Critical Things During Validation Process
- Know The 6 Buckets Of Your Idea Validation
- Prefer Working In Your Areas Of Interest
- Insource Your Ability Area Work, Outsource Your Weak Areas
- **Answer Cleary** : Who, Why, When, Where, What & How ?
- There Are No Shortcuts To Success
- Try Business Model Canvas Approach
- Build A Product Life Cycle Board
- Forget Spreadsheets If You Want, Work Practical
- Have Customers Who Will Work With You
- Do Your Market Research To Get Realistic Data
- Build A MVP/Prototype, Go To Market, Early, Fast
- Hire A Mentor Or Advisor On Board
- Don't Rush Into Things
- Trust Diligently On Everyone
- Hire Teams Only When You Need Them
- Choose The Right Co-Founders
- Better To Have Competent Human Capital
- Build The Right Legal Documentation During Validation
- Talk To Existing Entrepreneurs, Take Feedbacks
- Do You Have The Ability To Pull Off The Business ?
- Know Your Market Entry Barriers
- Build Your Product/Services Roadmap
- Build Your Business Idea Board
- Reach Out To Your Networks
- Do You Have Clarity In What You Are Trying To Achieve ?
- Know Your Operational/Complete Breakeven
- You Should Know The Stage Of Funds For Sustenance

Real Time Assignment - Test Your Market/Business

Now since now you have a thorough understanding of validation of your business idea, you need to do the following and take this assignment in the following steps :

1. Write down the USP of your Business Idea
2. Validate it with the right Target Audience
3. Build your own product life cycle board
4. Plan your list of prospective customers whom you want to pitch
5. Take your MVP/POC to them
6. Take realistic feedbacks
7. Ask them whether they are willing to pay for your product/service ?
8. How much ? Is your pricing fine ?
9. Product/Service improvement feedback ?
10. Go back improve the product/service
11. Rinse, Repeat
12. Now, Build a soft GTM planning
13. Set up some real time deadlines, pitstops
14. Set some goals
15. Go through the last chapter and take some notes
16. Now you are ready to move ahead

Keep in mind you are prepared for the next level. Once you have crossed it you can get to the next level and get to the Post Business Validation Mindset.

The next part will help you to build a strong and viable growth oriented business in tough times which will cover all your fears and questions on a broader level.

Post Business Validation Mindset
Key Pointers That Can Help You Bounce Back & Grow

Let's Unlearn & Relearn.

"

Building Growth & Bouncing Back In Tough Times Is A Combination Of Unlearning & Relearning Processes Followed By An Eager Sense Of Structuring The Business With Clarity, Hope & A Strong Desire To Lead With A Purpose By Betting On The Future.

Ravi Kikan

Startup Basics While We Dig Deep

Unlearn & Relearn

#StartupTips #RaviSupportMyStartup

Rinse Repeat
You Are NOT Building A Product
You Are Building A Business
#RaviSupportMyStartup

Startup Tip 1

You Are Building A Business. Remember That.

This is not about just the product and service you are trying to launch or build.

Now since you have covered the validation process for your business this is the most important thing that you need to keep in mind. Time and again I have had millions of conversations with aspiring entrepreneurs, students, successful startups and enterprise builders and one thing came out clearly all the time.

Always keep the broad picture in mind.

So, What's that broad picture ?

There is one thing you should always remember about these two points when you are building a product or a service.

1.   You are not building JUST a product or a service
2.   You are building a whole damn business

Oxymoron isn't it ?

This would mean you would have to look beyond just building your product, validating it in the right market or for that matter going out to find new customers who want to buy your product/services.

You would also have to look at building your able human capital line up, your financial projections, your marketing planning, your sales strategy, your recruitment and hiring processes, your business and culture that would define you. The entire business end to end.

If you do not have the expertise in any of the functions either hire people who can do it for you or take expert opinion or outsource to some professionals so that you can focus on the key things you are good at.

These are equally important and critical things to be looked into.

Building a great product or service and validating is just the tip of the iceberg. The real work starts after that & it goes real deep.

Keep in mind before you jump all out.

Startup Tip 2

Identifying The Right Target Audience (TA)

Here is something everyone who wants to market their product or service should ideally know. This is irrespective of whether you are in a Startup or an Enterprise. This is a prelude to real market dynamics & building your GTM (Go To Market) Planning.

Before you plan your GTM, go through & think like your ideal Target Audience and suddenly your marketing will be more effective , more focussed and more direct.First thing is the mix of the target audience to whom we are addressing, this is the categorization from a birth point of view and how they are called.

You need to know this because identifying the TA ensures you can build a smooth product/service that the customer might really need or want. Knowing the TA becomes critical.

Why are they called like this ?

Well they show traits in a particular order. Generic generation gaps that we all see across. You know what I mean now when we talk about our dads, granddads and the olders generations. This is how they are called with respect to the timelines when they were born.

- Post-War Cohort. 1928-1945
- Baby Boomers. 1946-1954
- Boomers II 1955-1965
- Generation X. 1966-1976
- Millenniums. 1977-1994
- Generation Z. 1995-2012

The second thing is the SEC (Socio Economic Categorization) which builds the real funnel of your target audience base.Keep in mind these 2 things both from a B2B & B2C perspective. This comes very handy.

(Credits: Internet & wikipedia)

OCCUPATION \ EDUCATION		Illiterate	Literate but no formal schooling	School upto 4 years	School 5 to 9 years	SSC / HSC	Some College but not graduate	Graduate / Post Graduate - General	Graduate / Post Graduate – Professional
Unskilled Worker		E2	E2	E2	E1	D	D	D	D
Skilled Worker		E2	E1	E1	D	C	C	B2	B2
Petty Trader		E2	D	D	D	C	C	B2	B2
Shop Owner		D	D	D	C	B2	B1	A2	A2
Businessmen / Industrialist – (No. of employees)	None	D	C	C	B2	B1	A2	A2	A1
	1-9	C	B2	B2	B2	B1	A2	A1	A1
	10+	B1	B1	B1	A2	A2	A1	A1	A1
Self Employed Professional		D	D	D	D	B2	B1	A2	A1
Clerical / Salesman		D	D	D	D	C	B2	B1	B1
Supervisory Level		D	D	D	C	C	B2	B1	A2
Officers / Executives – Junior		C	C	C	C	B2	B1	A2	A2
Officers / Executives – Middle / Senior		B1	B1	B1	B1	B1	A2	A1	A1

Rinse Repeat

Be Good At Many
Be Awesome At One

@ravikikan

#RaviSupportMyStartup

Startup Tip 3

Be Awesome At Least One Thing

What is the best job or service to work for ?

You should be good at doing a lot of things and learning new ones, Yes I agree & that's fine. While you might be good at many levels and functions there is always a brilliant way of seeing things and understanding that one thing.

What is that one thing that you are amazing at ? That one thing that you are awesome at. Think.

That one thing is your calling, your expertise which no one has or very few will have it. Be good at many levels and do many things but be awesome at doing that one thing. That one thing will help you build up the momentum.

e.g. **for pre validation mindset**

1. You love art , have you explored being an artist ? You don't need a degree for that
2. You are awesome at networking, have you explored taking this professionally ?
3. You are brilliant at sales, have you thought of aligning to align with someone who needs you ?
4. You are super in writing but stuck in sales, have you explored writing content for startups ?
5. You see an opportunity, a market gap and you are great in building products, what are you waiting for ?

If you have launched your business the most critical thing is what you are awesome at in doing for your business.

DO NOT handle everything that you can't do properly. You might want to oversee them but not lead them, let your team or co-founders do it.

e.g. **for scaling up and growth mindset**

You are looking at growth marketing and you have a great understanding of product but not marketing. Make sure you work on the product and make sure the product experience is awesome so you either outsource your marketing or hire someone to help you market your product/service.

Focus on your strengths and outsource your weakness to someone who might have those strengths whether internal or external human capital.

Keep in mind the trial and error theory works fine if you have all the money and time in the world to experiment. However if you have a thin deadline it is always better that you keep & drive the competencies and outsource everything out.

Smart people do that. Be smart.

Rinse Repeat.

Focus On The Need
Pitch Smart

@ravikikan

#RaviSupportMyStartup

Startup Tip 4

Building The Right POV (Point of View)

We are often told and sometimes directed to pitch a whole Presentation/PPT to prospective customers or investors or stakeholders at large. Whether you are a startup, smb or an enterprise you have a defined model for pitching. We lose deals because of this, this cuts your scale up plans.

You are TOLD so, We all are TOLD so :)

It is easy, you dump the entire load of whatever your venture, startup, enterprise or smb has done so far in a PPT format and go ahead and share.Very few resist but mostly follow. Most of the folks just do the Ctrl C & Ctrl V process time and again.

The objective is then to write a whole damn mail and a bulky 10 MB presentation which never reaches the prospect or gets dumped in his junk or for that matter never opened even if sent.

Honestly no one wants to see a 10 MB file of your product or service demo.

So, What changes in time actually ?

The fonts, design, color palette or the content perhaps of the PPT.

What doesn't change in time ?

The Damn PPT :)

Strongly suggest or recommend pitch a solution in the shortest/smartest possible way to any of the stakeholders or prospects. Address the need, maybe build a smart infographic or a video pitch.

e.g. Share a Link or Send a Smart explainer video on a website or a dynamic infographic to pitch your product. Remember 10 million people are doing the same thing as you are doing.

So what next ?

Excite the prospect, stakeholder by pitching something interesting, keep it short, keep it simple, keep it crisp. This is a growth mindset.

You save time, you reach out to a bigger audience, you reach fast.

Startup Tip 5

Strong User Experience & Design Thinking

The first set of questions that you need to understand and ask before designing or building any product or service are :

- *" How Will The Customer or the TA (Target Audience) Use This ? "*
- *" How Can I Make It Super Easy For My TA ? "*
- *" Is It Super Handy ? "*
- *" How Much Effort Will It Take From The Customer ? "*
- *" Why Should He or She Buy Only This and From Us ? "*
- *" How Often & Quickly Can The Customer Use This ? "*

You can put most of these questions for anything or any product, whether it is a SaaS or a physical product. The rest of the questions like actual Design User Interface etc can be worked upon later but first address the elephant in the house.

Building the customer journey has to be focussed more than anything else. Spend the maximum time with your team/cofounders to get this done.

An easy & excellent UX is a valid success benchmark.

If you have already launched your product/services, it might not be a bad idea to revisit your UX time and again and improve it based on your TA feedback. This is the sweetest reason why people buy products/services quickly and the prospective customer dropout is less.

How can I make life real easy for my customers so that they can seamlessly buy ?

As this question time and again

Great User Experience for the Target Audience.Design Thinking does that on many levels to build with Agile and Lean thinking

Rinse Repeat
Offering Quality
Ultimate Marketing
@ravikikan
#RaviSupportMyStartup

Startup Tip 6

Focus On The HIGH Customer Experience (CX) & Quality Delivery

Once you have done formulating and understanding your target market, built your product and launched in the market, keep in mind these following things :

1. Your MRR (Monthly Recurring Revenue) from paying customers is pivotal.
2. Your existing customers are to be retained and they become your brand ambassadors for life
3. You need to focus on the overall Customer Experience not just selling and marketing your product
4. It is better to have 10 regular paying customers than have 100 paying customers coming to you once and not coming back for repeat buy
5. Remember your product or service quality speaks a volume about how a customer will remember you, keep that quality super high.
6. Focus on the repeat buy, recurring business, MRR

In these tough times I have been working with some awesome entrepreneurs and I have seen it time and again , the ones who have focussed on Customer Experience for new customers as well as old customers are the ones you are floating in these torrid times.This is a mandatory part of any founders manual. The way we look at sales, marketing & tech....Customer Experience becomes a pivotal part of the hub and spoke model of the business.

Customer Experience is a sum and substance of creating & building

- Engagement
- Experience
- Purchase
- Delivery
- Prompting Repeat Buy
- Organic Testimonials

Customer Experience Cycle

Growth Marketing Basics

Clear USP
Honest POV
Content Aligned With TA
Build Great Product Recall
Amazing Thought Leadership

@ravikikan

#RaviSupportMyStartup

Startup Tip 7

Growth Marketing Basics You Should Understand

Product or Service selling through marketing initiatives is more of an art than handling a function. The faster you realize the better you become at doing this.

The understanding of a Growth Marketing mindset can be divided into the following elements :

- Having a well defined USP (Unique Selling Proposition)
- Having an honest POV (Point Of View)
- Your content should be aligned with your TA (Target Audience)
- Creating a great product recall among the TA (Target Audience)
- Building & Creating an awesome Thought Leadership

Let me explain each of these briefly with an example so that you can quickly understand say e.g. a healthcare/healthtech startup which is planning to launch a smart wrist watch that can detect your Blood Sugar at any point in time.

Well defined USP	" This watch will show your blood sugar "
Honest POV	" If we don't deliver in 48 hours, the product is free "
Content/TA	Pitching a Diabetic Product to a 25 Vs a 52 year old
Product Recall	" That brand watch shows blood sugar so easily "
Thought Leadership	How to control & check your blood sugar super easily.

Focus on the basic, keep it simple & direct.

Always remember people align with products and services they feel connected to. The objective of a growth marketing mindset is to quickly trigger that want in the customer for an instant buy.

Keep in mind the following things whenever you are building a smart marketing plan :

- Where is my TA located ?
- How will I reach fast to my TA ?

- What is the best medium to reach them fast ?
- When is the right time to reach them fast ?
- Why will he or she consume my data or content ?
- Who will get this entire GTM (Go To Market) planning & execution done ?
- How will I measure my reach and success ?
- What is the outcome I am looking for e.g. in Brand Recall among stakeholders/Thought Leadership/ More quality leads/More product or service awareness.

Rinse Repeat

Build The Business For Yourself
Not The Investor

@ravikikan

#RaviSupportMyStartup

Startup Tip 8

You build the business for yourself & growth.

Many entrepreneurs from the very start plan to build the business keeping only the exit in mind.

Their entire working is on the pretext of how we will sell the business to a bigger VC or investor.

WRONG.

These entrepreneurs who focus too much on the exit perspective have their entire focus of sales, marketing, growth etc keeping only the future investor in mind and not primarily the business growth per se. This thinking has to come once you have reached the growth curve and you are expanding the business in the maturity stage to grow with leaps and bounds and not in the very start of your business.

I have had many conversations with startups, aspiring entrepreneurs, investors and experts and this is one thing that came out Loud & Clear. You might completely disagree, that's fair :)

However the real reason why you start or scale a business is for growing the idea into a viable, sustainable and game changing solution. The idea of the investor coming in is primarily for scaling up and not for him or her to buy your business (if that happens eventually that's a great thing but that shouldn't be the motive of your starting or scaling your business)

I mean in the whole journey of you playing with your business the entry of any strategic investor is cool but keep in mind that you are not building it for him or her. Focus on your business validation, sustainability and growth first beyond anything or anyone else. So this means when you expanding your business or growing it keep these following things in mind most of the time :

1. Building Break Even Fast
2. Focus on Your Operating Capital Needs

3. Hanging On To Your Existing Customers
4. Acquiring Customers Fast To Hit Breakeven
5. Focus On Organic Reach & Marketing
6. Don't Wait For The Perfect Product version, Launch As On Where On Basis
7. Don't Think About The Investor While Building Your Plans
8. Focus On Product + Customer Mix

In my honest opinion please do not start building your matrix keeping the exit options in mind, please focus on the growth and building your business.

A lot of your precious energy, time, money will be wasted if you choose this path of running behind investors for an exit play. Infact lot of smart investors also understand this and they smell it real fast. So instead of travelling to a road which might never take you to your destination please prepare for a road that might just take you to your business goals.

Rinse Repeat
Pivot Fast
Pivot Smart
#RaviSupportMyStartup

Startup Tip 9

A Smart Entrepreneur Always Pivots Fast & Smart

Let us understand a situation where either of thing has happened

1. The demand for your business has slowed down
2. There is no demand for your product or service e.g. in Covid19 times
3. Someone has come up in the market with a better offering
4. You are left behind on the innovation curve

There are two outcomes that you can choose :

1. Give up and curse your luck/times
2. Stand up and deal with it

I would suggest and highly recommend the second outcome. In Fact that only. There is a reason for the same and let me give you some examples.

During these unforeseen times like Covid19 when the entire world went into lockdown at numerous levels and times, a lot of small and medium sized businesses got hit. However some of these businesses quickly pivoted into some other business vertical, Why ?

There was a demand for that new business. So what did they do ?

They Pivoted Their Business, Fast and Smart. Of Course they did not completely change their line of business but added new assembly lines for products or services. Here are some examples :

1. Lot of breweries around the world started making hand sanitizers. Smart move. The basic ingredients of a sanitizer is primarily alcohol based. So it was just changing packaging and product lines to build the same. Demand has been huge so pivoting came handy.

2. Lot of fashion houses which had been selling luxury items pivoted into building PPEs & Face masks. The assembly line remained the same, the product changed. The demand has been huge.
3. Lot of food delivery & food tech companies started delivering essential food items rather than just packed and processed foods as during the lockdowns the demand for essential food items was higher as compared to processed or restaurant based food. Plus the chains for home delivery of food had been massively hit with the restrictions, containment and lockdown.

Remember to pivot your business fast and smart.

Time is the essence here. Keep that in mind only one thing. You focus on the demand and need of the market, you can always come back doing what you did before but as of now and in tough times remember to address the current market and be future ready to pivot again with time.

Rinse Repeat
Work Lean & Agile
@ravikikan
#RaviSupportMyStartup

The Right Mindset Team Player

Problem Solver
Progressive
Patient
Peer Loving

@RAVIKIKAN

#RaviSupportMyStartup

Startup Tip 10

Small Team, Smarter Team, Flexible Team

Human Capital is the base of growth and sustenance of any startup across the globe. The right team is always responsible for getting things done.

In tough and challenging times, the best saviour is your business model and your able team. Yes a small amount of luck is also required, I wouldn't deny that. Let us understand what kind of team comes handy and why you need to relook at this.

What is a lean and agile team ?

A small all rounding team which is flat in structure and multitasking to start with.

Lean Team
Quick Decisions, Faster Actions, Flat Structures In Reporting

Agile Team
Super Collaborative, Communicative, Problem Solving Ability With Quick Iterations

There are some key traits that you need to build within your team or for that matter ensure that you pick a lean and agile team with these traits 4 key traits :

1. Problem Solving Mindset
2. Progressive Thinking
3. Perspective of Patience
4. Peer Loving & Collaborative

Keep in mind either you can groom your current team inot this growth and progressive mindset or you have to hire people who can fit into the maximum buckets of the above traits.

Most likely the right and able human capital will not only back up the venture but will be self driven to get things done at times when you need them most to deliver and to perform. The right teams only need directions to get things done and this brings in the right kind of framework to build that leap towards faith.

Tough times or unforseen times of turmoil need a more cohesive team that works and wins together and supports each other to bring the real deals on the table and not waste time in negative thinking or approach.

You might not get a real perfect team but it is ok to have a current aligned team which you can train in the various competencies to get work done. I have seen time and again great entrepreneurs and successful startups building and nurturing their teams for tough times and unprecedented times.

These are the times when they rise and support the bigger objective of business and well being.

Startup Tip 11

When you don't ask , Most likely the answer is always a **BIG NO**

Here is how our startup community on Linkedin is helping small business owners & supporting entrepreneurship in all ways we can. You can go to the startup community Startup Specialists on Linkedin and look at the "Recommended" section post to check details.

The best part of doing this outreach is that you get to work with some amazing & extraordinarily brilliant people & entrepreneurs globally in supporting them in highlighting them and their businesses.

Here is one of them, Amy HAMMOND did reach out to her network and she was highlighted in the global community of 400,000+ startup specialists. Ask for help and most likely you will get help. Amy reached out, she got help from the community.

This is a classic case in example which you will find in the below mentioned screenshot.

Be like Amy

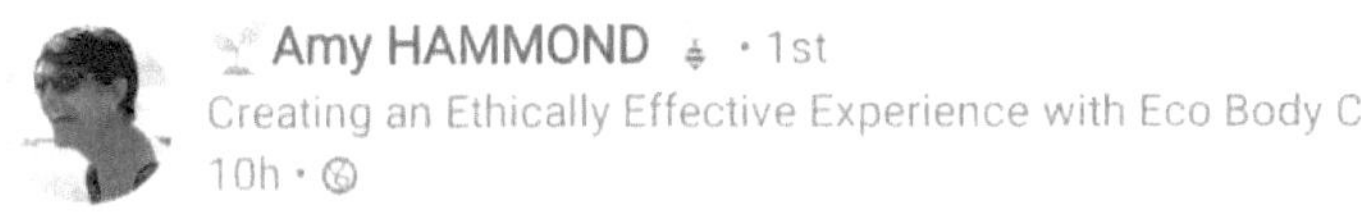

Hi to my LinkedIn family and friends!

Ravi has shown up for me and many others and if you know me at all, you know I sincerely cherish supporting my network however you see most fitting.

When an opportunity reveals itself, like today, in joining one of Ravi Kikan's start up groups, I am honored to pay it forward.

Tracey Kitching
Kerryn Zwag
Alessio Rinaldo

#RaviSupportMyStartup

Be well. Be happy.
Amy

A STARTUP SPECIALISTS GROUP Online Global Network for Entrepreneurs,Startups (Business ...

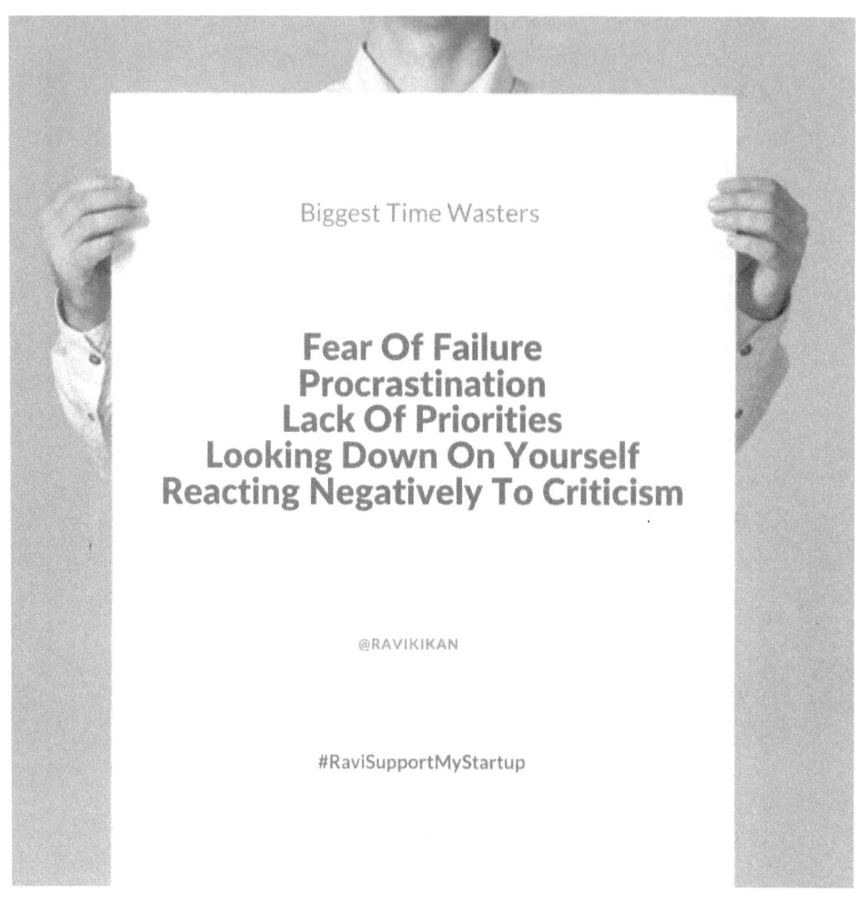

Biggest Time Wasters

Fear Of Failure
Procrastination
Lack Of Priorities
Looking Down On Yourself
Reacting Negatively To Criticism

@RAVIKIKAN

#RaviSupportMyStartup

Startup Tip 12

Biggest Time Wasters For Anyone, Anytime

Keep in mind that your time is limited and when you are in tough times or situations you shouldnt ideally spend that time in repenting or in negative mindsets.These are the top time wasters which you should always avoid for self, teams and everyone around you so as to keep a positive outlook in mind and soul.

So avoid :

1. Thinking about fear of failure
2. Procrastination
3. Not building a list of priorities for self or business
4. Looking down of yourself
5. Reacting to people or circumstances in a negative way

So let's take some examples :

Thinking about fear of failure
Thought :   " These are tough times, if I launch the product I will fail"
Remedy :   " Have you Validated your product business idea ? "

Procrastination
Thought :   " I need to delay this launch, I do not know how to market"
Remedy :   " Have you tried content marketing or hiring an intern "

Not building a list of priorities for self or business
Thought :   " There is so much to do, where should I start now ?"
Remedy :   " Have you tried making a list of priorities across functions "

Looking down of yourself

Thought :	" I am not from Ivy League, I do not have funds, I am useless"

Remedy :	" Do you know that there is only 1 person in the world with your DNA "

Reacting to people or circumstances in a negative way

Thought :	" I don't think you are cut out for entrepreneurship, you are too soft "

Remedy :	" If you have a product market fit and a paying customer, why not "

Growth Mindset
Accelerate Acquisition
Strong Customer Retention
Product/Service Innovation
Building Scale
#RaviSupportMyStartup

Startup Tip 13

The Real Growth Mindset

This is the real deal for you to adopt a growth mindset and build your team for the same. With my own experience from working with awesome entrepreneurs, startups and learning from brilliant leaders, all had this growth mindset in common.

The growth mindset is all about this :

How would you quickly scale up the organization and business as a whole ?

This is about doing the following things :

1. Increasing the top & bottom line
2. Creating profitability
3. Productivity and Outcomes are critical
4. Building a team which thinks on the same lines
5. Have realistic pitstop which are measurable
6. Building a USP for your product/services
7. Market your product/service smartly
8. Focus on un orthodox channels for marketing and outreach

How does a growth mindset change the course of action for your business ?

1. It accelerates customer acquisition which is the key
2. Focusses on your MRR (Monthly Recurring Revenue)
3. Helps you focus on existing customer retention
4. Builds a solid customer experience program through channels like CSAT (Customer Satisfaction Scores)
5. Builds a scalable business
6. Builds a team which can focus on the growth and retention

More often than not your understanding of the growth mindset has to be put in perspective and pit stops for growth have to be made more tangible and outcome focussed.

e.g. We will do X million in sales in this quarter with Y% spent in marketing through these following channels and get to a Z MRR. The team structure to get this done will be focussed with tangible outcomes to be measured WOW (Week on Week) basis.

This also builds a short term and long term objective for your business which in any case will be addressed and taken care of by the functional and management teams when you do both the macro and micro level planning of milestones and tangible outcomes.

Bounce Back Basics - Revision

Here is a basic revision of the key pointers that we went through in the last chapters on what will be the key elements when you are either bouncing back, relaunching or building scale for your business in anytimes specially the tough and unprecedented times.

These tips were not born from the skies :)

On a serious note these tips are hard earned from million experiences time and again. These are also the most important things that any entrepreneur should keep in mind when he or she is trying to build a business or is the process of scaling his or her business at any point in time and anywhere for that matter.

People have tried, tested and still failed when they have repeated mistakes time and again which they shouldn't. The growth mindset also ensures the fear of failure of scaling up your venture is minimized in the whole process and a streamlined process to reach your tangible goals is built.

Here are the key things you should remember:

1. Remember you are building a business and not just a product/service
2. Identifying the right target audience (TA) is super critical
3. Be awesome at one thing and do that brilliantly
4. Building the right POV(Point of view)
5. Strong user experience and design thinking mindset is critical
6. High customer experience and quality focus is always required
7. Growth marketing basics should be taken care
8. You are building a business for self and NOT the investor
9. Pivot fast & Pivot smart, this comes handy in tough times
10. Have a right growth team, you have think and act like that
11. Work Lean & Agile, Things are better and faster this way
12. When you don't ask for help, the answer is always NO
13. Avoid the biggest time wasters, Don't waste time on them

14. Have a real and tangible growth mindset, have realistic pit stops

Now since you are well equipped in your journey of building your mindset for bouncing back and growth let us also look at some suggestions and advice from some global rockstar entrepreneurs and experts on how to bounce back in tough times.

These suggestions might just help you in getting a new perspective altogether.

Global Point Of View

Road Ahead In Tough Times

These are tough times however rockstars who can dream of seeing the future will sail through these tough times. The speed of bounce back is massive if you can sail through tough times.

As I shared before I also invited some awesome startup specialists, entrepreneurs, mentors, VCs and global experts to share their point of view on this topic. The reason why I took a diverse opinion was to understand the different points of view in the startup ecosystem.

It is imperative for you as a reader to understand that taking an opinion on a subject from experts from various sectors across the globe gives you a perspective from almost all corners that you might have not seen or thought of. Not all options lead to success however if we take a diverse view chances of failure gets reduced drastically and with some more focus & knowledge (that you gain from experts) you might as well taste success on the way :)

The objective for assimilating myriad thoughts from across the world is to help you build your business in a very clear, crisp and uniform fashion so that whatever startup you are planning to get into, you get a complete perspective. You might be a student, homemaker, professional from the corporate world, a budding entrepreneur, someone who has already conceptualized his idea to launch as a business, a retired professional or anyone who has jumped into the chaotic world of startups or or someone who has already launched his or her business, there is only one thing that always comes handy to you. **Advices & Lots Of It**.

There is no harm taking advice. In fact it is absolutely necessary that the more advice you take from people from across regions, geographies, sectors, levels and functions, the more chances are that you will get a more holistic view for your startup business idea. You will be surprised that some of the suggestions, situations, ideas etc you would have never imagined at all and would have never prepared yourself and your venture for the same.

Stay prepared for the unknown & **KILL the fear of the Unknown** and that's the reason why I always reach out to people, experts to take their opinion to get a different perspective of the same thing that I am thinking.

Keep your notepad and your pen ready to take down notes of each and every new point that you would have not thought about your venture and keep the perspective lighted up with various thoughts and situations.

" Tell Me & I Will Forget,
* Show Me & I May Remember,*
Involve Me & I Learn"
---- Benjamin Franklin

AI & Healthcare: Post Covid-19 Challenges & Opportunities

Dr. Ramchander Chepyala
Co-Founder and Scientist

Dr. Ram Chepyala obtained a Ph.D. from IIT Kanpur, an M.Tech from the IIT Madras, and a B.Tech from NIT Warangal, all in Chemical Engineering. He did his postdoc in microfluidics and biosensors from IIT Bombay and MIT, USA prior to joining as a Scientific Researcher at FPC@DCU at DCU, Ireland. His research focuses on chemical sensors, microfluidics, lab on chip technologies and the accompanying transport, reactions. He published several scientific articles, book chapters and filed five patent applications. He is a co-founder of GATE counsellor, a web platform to promote higher education in India and scibash.com that helps in providing information on funding, investment, relief and similar opportunities to start-ups.

www.linkedin.com/in/dr-ram-chepyala
www.scibash.com

"Knowing is not enough, we must apply. Willing is not enough, we must do it."
-    Bruce Lee

Post Covid-19, technologies such as artificial intelligence (AI) and machine learning (ML) would revolutionize every possible sector including healthcare in an unimaginable way. The financial estimates based on the anticipated benefits of AI, ML shows mind-boggling numbers rising hopes for a better future. It is difficult to ignore the impact of these linear speculations about the future to some extent based on current available data and level of understanding.

However, the future is non-linear; hence, none of the technology giants, think tanks etc., neither predicted the possible emergence of Black Swans such as Covid-19 nor can surely suggest what kind of demands, challenges or disruptive technologies would emerge post Black Swan. Despite that, the projected investments in AI may go beyond $6 billion by 2021 and lead to annual savings more than $150 billion by 2026. In addition, to add fuel to the burning desire on

AI, all over the world smaller to larger organizations, universities including technology leaders such as MIT started investing as much as $1 billion to create colleges, centres to work on AI and computing.

Until Covid-19 declared as a pandemic, all over the world academia, industry actively focused on investing in R&D of AI, ML along with interdisciplinary areas for training NextGen workforce by offering degree programs, online courses and at the same time worked on trivial projects. Unfortunately, this pandemic hit the world so badly that we left with no other option except to urgently start working on the most important challenges in the domain of healthcare and related sectors to innovate and implement realistic solutions. There is no doubt that the implementation of AI, ML in healthcare would immediately lead to impact in streamlining the management operations, administrative tasks, seamless patient flow, bookkeeping, registrations, tracking etc., compared to the projected role of AI on precision surgery, automation of clinical operations, drug development, preventive interventions or diagnostics and EMR.

It is evident that the development of an efficient, robust yet simple diagnostic technology device (not software, Apps) at an affordable cost not necessarily be user-friendly for molecular detection of diseases beyond pregnancy test kits, glucose kits not yet realized despite more than five decades of interest and four decades of rigorous R&D. Moreover, huge investments from the public and private sectors including philanthropic agencies pushed into the academic, industrial R&Ds across the world for developing such molecular detection kits/devices for various diseases.

Despite, several proposed platform technologies failed to see the light of the day and hardly succeeded beyond the walls of the labs. Therefore, the questions remain to be answered are, are we not capable of creating workable technologies. Are we not doing the right science? If at all, we are doing everything right then what are those factors limiting these technologies to reach the market? Post pandemic, there would be a storm of AI based solutions in healthcare, which create intense pressure on the scientific community in both academia and industry to develop workable diagnostic or related technologies at unprecedented pace. It also forces to amend the existing or create new technologies to accommodate AI, ML based modules for addressing the intended services.

One can also see rise in AI based predictive interventions in diagnostics, where mobile Apps promises to address every possible problem of the patients. In addition, AI based predictive interventions domain attracts significant investments. The flipside of it is that it may lead to many inferior devices/technologies flooding the market from back doors claiming to be the best AI based solutions that might not be scientifically validated or meet the regulations.

The false outcomes from such devices would rob the trust of the users leading to the loss of credibility on potential technologies such as AI, ML, and point of care diagnostics kits. Therefore, the question remains, does AI is a boon or a bane when it robs the trust of the users, causes mental distress due to false diagnosis, and additionally causes financial loss along with loss of valuable time.

In the end, post-covid-19 pushes us to think innovative ways to translate the science into workable solutions and upgrade conventional technologies/devices/tools to meet the emergencies with provision for AI, ML based modules for predictive solutions without breaching the patient's private data.

Synopsis in 5 Points.

1. AI and ML revolutionize the healthcare and related domains Post-Covid-19
2. Integration of AI, ML with the diagnostic technologies would be the game changer
3. Significant investment opportunities in AI based predictive interventions in diagnostics
4. AI based predictive intervention Apps must be scientifically validated and should meet regulatory aspects.
5. Post-Covid-19 brings the paradigm shift in translating science into workable solutions.

We've achieved $10M ARR, 100% Bootstrapped

Shalin Jain
Entrepreneur. Built multiple successful product companies. Design & product
focused founder. Tesla fanboy.

I am a CEO with a customer success game plan. I have worked with C-level
executives and managers to analyze, plan and implement a great customer service
program by bringing adequate centralization, transparency, metrics and tools.I am
a designer at heart, passionate about crafting beautiful products and working with
great people.

https://www.linkedin.com/in/shalinjain
Happyfox.com

It took us 7 years to go from 100k to $10M. Been an incredible journey and here
are the highlights.

I want to thank my team for their hard work. I want to thank our customers who
have grown with us and put their trust behind us. Also, sincere gratitude towards
my mentors, family, friends, vendors, and all employees past and present who
have helped me and HappyFox get here.While this is an important milestone for
us – this is not really what drives us. Revenue and growth-rate are by-products of
a great product and team. We will continue to work very hard to execute our
vision – transforming experiences for customer support leading to happier
customers.

We are actually trying to sell to less people (I know sounds strange) and want
customers to start the conversation when time is right for them. Our sales team is
small and the sales process is designed for conversion and reduced chatter. Trial to
Win is around 35%.

On the other hand our chat product has free trial and no sales touch. We also
achieved a 25-30% conv rate.While this is an important milestone for us - this is
not really what drives us. Revenue and growth-rate are by-products of a great

product and team.We will continue to work very hard and continue executing on our vision: transforming experiences for customer support leading to happier customers. We largely focused on our product and optimized for the bottom of our sales funnel.

Our story in numbers:

- We raised $0 in outside funding
- Our team size grew from 10 to 85
- We have grown ~70% YoY in the last 3 years
- We achieved a 96% CSAT score in 2019
- In 2019, we spent less than 6% of revenue on advertising
- Sales & Marketing represents less than 10% of company size
- We have stayed profitable all through our growth.
- Reached $10M in Q1 2020

Outcomation For Growth Bound Enterprises

Prasad Rajappan
MD & Founder

Prasad Rajappan is the Founder and MD of ZingHR - a Global Enterprise Cloud HR Applications provider aimed at simplifying Human Capital Management (HCM) catering to 1 Million Employee Records. ZingHR has been the driving force that is helping organizations go beyond Automation, and deliver a solution that could directly impact Business Outcomes - Outcomation™

A Firm Believer Of Delivering rather than Promising, Prasad has always looked at challenges as opportunities to grow. An active personality in the room who will always keep the ball rolling and getting the best out of time. He brings an experience of over 3 decades into ideating and putting a concept into action. He has held senior management positions in Mahindra & Mahindra, Ernst & Young and Reliance in Business Process Reengineering, Change Management, and SAP Projects. He was a part of the SAP Project Directorate at Reliance, which managed more than 30 SAP implementations across various industry verticals like Petrochemical, Energy, and Business Process Re-engineering. He has earned a Master's Degree in HR and Operations from Mumbai University, and a Bachelor's Degree in Production Engineering.

linkedin.com/in/prasad-rajappan-a002a73
www.zinghr.com

A lot of CEOs, CHRO's are saying Let us put AI, ML, Bots but research says **68%** of initiatives don't yield results because we are focusing on automation and not on **<u>Outcomation</u>**. We at ZingHR – Global HR Software Platform have coined the term 'Outcomation' which means, focusing on Business Outcomes through HR Innovations. We often mix up between, Activity and Productivity, Value-added and Non-Value Added, Purpose and Means. I strongly believe that HR should take up the role of strategic business partners and drive Business Outcomes for their organisations.

Adopt LEAN HR, Eliminate Non-Value Added Processes (NVA): In LEAN management methodology, all activities in an organisation are grouped into two categories viz., Value-added activities and Non-value added activities. These are as seen by the customer, both internal as well as external. HR teams often complain that they are so busy with mundane admin activities, that they do not get time to do real HR stuff. Working across several organisations, wherein we have oriented users towards a LEAN methodology, the findings for HR admin processes are that a mere 1% is the value-added activities, 23% are non-value added activities but currently essential, and 76% are non-value added activities but currently non-essential. Surprised? Or is it that you always knew, but were not realising the magnitude.

Technology is transforming traditional HR functions such as hiring and onboarding, learning and development, HR administration, however, Business Outcomation is the purpose: Let's focus on it. In today's world, the business has become dynamic and technology has become disruptive. We strongly believe Technology is the Means and not the Purpose. High employee engagement tends to have an improved business outcome, increases EBIDTA margins and customer satisfaction.

Team performance is given higher priority as compared to individual performance. It's an opportunity for everyone who believes in agility and adaptability. We as an HR Tech Business Partner believes that growing enterprises should focus on Customer Retention, Growth and most importantly business outcomes.

This becomes the purpose and the means is

1. How do I improve Productivity?
2. How do I upgrade my skills?
3. How do I get transparency built-in?
4. How do I show concern for my people?
5. Most importantly, how do I convert Fixed Cost to Variable Cost?
6. As managers, what can we do to achieve things?
7. How do we face realities of loss in revenue with costs remaining the same?

The **ZingHR Outcomation**™ model to contribute directly to your Business Goals and generate Impact through the adoption of its key drivers: Employee Engagement Index, Eliminating non-value Added processes, Robotic Process Automation, Insights Based Data.

Clarity of Purpose, Align teams for this larger purpose and drive it jointly with Passion and Perseverance till you achieve it.

HEART + HEAD + HANDS = RECIPE FOR SUCCESS

HEART: depicts the passion that one puts into a task
HEAD: depicts the brains that one uses for achieving a task
HANDS: depicts the efforts that you do to complete the task

Dr. Amrinder Kaur
Co-founder , Consultant and Researcher

I'm Dr.Amrinder Kaur (B.Tech, MBA, PhD) with more than 13 years of experience in various corporate and academic profiles. I work as a Consultant, Advisor, Researcher, and Mentor. I have also partnered and worked through a consultancy and training firm. We support organizations/entrepreneurs to create differentiation and growth strategies through Customer Experience Management (www.pinkguava.org). We do customize research studies involving process improvement, people engagement, policy interventions and customer feedback surveys along with strategic/vision support to entrepreneurs/organizations.

https://www.linkedin.com/in/kauramrinder
https://www.pinkguava.org/customerexperienceblogs

Do not wait; the time will never be "just right". Start where you stand, and work with whatever tools you may have at your command, and better tools will be found as you go long
-    Naploean Hill

Customer Engagement is the interaction a brand/company has with its customers. Engagement also defines in the depth of involvement of the customer with the brand/company, as per the customer's convenience. And this typically involves careful & thoughtful approaches by the brand/company through regular evaluation, measurement, and improvement.

A business is because of the customers and hence customer engagement is equally or rather very important even for startups irrespective of whether they are in their initial stages of growth or in their normal day to day functioning, or maybe even while scaling up.

Through customer engagements only, a startup or brand builds its differentiating Customer Experience, and great customer experience also in turns supports further in building greater engagement with customers. A thoughtfully designed engagement which is seamless with lesser effort for the customer will support. Customer Engagement will not only enhance customer loyalty but will also support to attract more customers.

And this all is good at regular times. But in unprecedented times like COVID, the question arises
1. All want more business and work – will customer engagement make a difference.
2. The customer himself/herself is going through challenges and hence, where is the time with customers to engage with a startup/brand.
3. Lack of finances means a muted demand scenario particularly with a lot of industries and sectors that are at standstill, in this scenario how does customer engagement make a difference ?
4. Isn't customer engagement just a marketing tactic?

Well, customer engagement is well beyond a marketing tactic. It is purposefully driven strategies that will support a company/brand to not only have loyal customers but will also support to get more referrals. And it is true for the times when all is great but more important for the tough times.

Yes, in the times of COVID-19 when all want more business, customer engagement will support startups or any organization to survive and thrive. Customer Engagement essentially means that the start-up is engaging with the customer which will lead to an emotional connection. The start-up if it is making efforts to reach out to customers with empathy and thoughtful approaches, will make customers reach out today or tomorrow for that particular product/service or maybe they will tell their friends/relatives more about it. This is also an opportunity for up-selling or cross-selling too.

The biggest problem in these times is the lack of clarity about the current status of the availability of different goods/services. So customer engagement can also mean that a communication strategy is made to make the customers know that this particular product/service is available. And precautions are being taken with utmost planning in consideration of customer's health and security. Thus, customer engagement is done to build the trust, assurance, and comfort of the customer with the start-up for that particular product/service.

Maybe the product/service of the start-up is an essential, a necessity –then engaging with customers during these times will mean

1. To let them know if there will be a delay in deliveries or the expectations customers should have with respect to deliverables.
2. Or information regarding a startup's offering about particular product/service specifically
3. OR maybe communication with better offers to support in these times.

Even if a startup's product is a luxury and not a necessity, it is more pertinent to continue engaging to be in the customer's memory. Empathy is the key and so is a seamless experience. Building trust and working consistently to add value will go a long way in retaining and attracting more customers.

Customer Engagement is more than marketing; it is a strategy that involves careful integration of policies, processes, people, and product/service for a seamless experience. It is also true that customers have varied expectations and personalities and hence the engagement for an optimum needs careful design and consideration by the organization.

Typically, a customer is interacting through varied channels with the startup, for instance like website, app, social media, etc. Few actions which can support a startup to engage with their customers for greater success particularly in the times of COVID are listed below. There is a tremendous shift in customer behavior which altering the business models but few essentials remain the same,

1. The customer is both internal and external. Internal is the startup's employees, stakeholders whilst external are the actual users/consumers. It is equally important to support and engage the internal customers by understanding their challenges and supporting so they can add value through their work. So it means not an occasional engagement but thoughtful feedback, communication on how the business is going on, and what to expect as the start-up continues to tread the path in the future.

2. Engaging with end users/customers through a seamless, interactive, and above all consistent Omni-channel experience will need an understanding/mapping of customer expectations and start-up deliverables or value add.
3. Customer Journey Maps are an excellent source to understand customers from where the customer is coming, his emotions at different touch points, and the experience they are getting. Each customer touch point should be evaluated for the experience which is not only intuitive but has lesser customer effort. And thus it will need coordination of the people, policies with processes for a seamless experience
4. Analytics will come handy to support decision making for greater engagement/interaction. Along with different sales data, feedback (transactional/cumulative), customer behavior including real-time trends through social media, customer care, etc can help startups/brands to quantify the customer engagement and thus create an engaging and differentiating experience.
5. Benchmarking and finding the opportunities to improve will support creating more personalized offerings and programs for enhanced engagement and hence business success.

COVID-19 or any other challenging time is an opportunity to look and evaluate how a start-up or organization had been doing. Customer engagement can support business continuity. Customer engagement will ensure that the startups will have customers and it means the business will happen.

Synopsis in 5 Points.

1. Understanding customer engagement.
2. Importance of customer engagement.
3. Features of customer engagement.
4. Importance of customer engagement in times of COVID.
5. Achieving and enhancing customer engagement in the times of COVID.

Technology Essentials For Startups

Deepak Kikan
Tech Geek, Technology Enthusiast

A Post Graduate in Business Administration (major in marketing), Engineering graduate in Computer Science and a PMP with over 21 years of experience in various roles including Program Management consulting, Organizational Change Management Consulting, Program and Project Management, Agile Coach, SCRUM Master, Application support services delivery and Business Development. Currently responsible for Enterprise Digital Transformation Programs, PMO and Organizational Change Management implementation across the globe.

https://www.linkedin.com/in/deepakkikan

Technology plays a key role in differentiating a startup from a winner in the short and long term. It should be the focus of the board and it is imperative to have tech savvy people in the key positions. They not only understand the technology but can also drive the startup through the world of technical maze. They also make a better impression for the startup during the product presentations and demo for investor meetings.

Technology is so important that if you look around the major companies in the world are technology companies; Google, Facebook, Amazon, Apple, NetFlix and so many others. Even companies from the earlier era that were into traditional businesses are moving towards being the technology companies for example Reliance with the launch of Jio, fiber optics and now collaboration with Facebook is going digital in every aspect possible.

Every startup in the digital world is primarily a technical company with the domain business as the secondary for example, amazon is a technical company that is into retail or ecommerce, Uber is a technology company that is into the transportation business.

Considering these, here are few essentials for startups from technology perspective:

1. Cloud-first strategy: "Clouds bring rain and rains bring prosperity" is an old saying and apt for the startups for sure. The startups of the future should consider "Cloud first" as their key technical strategy. What it means is that any and all work that the startup does is done on the cloud. While it might incur initial costs but the benefits are enormous. I have heard and read many instances where the product was either sabotaged in the internal systems or the machine crashed a day before the investor met.
2. Security: The startups these days may become internally operating within no time and face the challenges of different regulations around security policies and concerns from the investors as well as from the users. So, it makes sense that the product is architected in a way that it is either compliant to the markets it is intended to be launched or is future-ready for such implementation. The cost of retro-fitting security is huge and in the meanwhile the startup may lose business and investors.
3. Privacy: Data privacy as well as user information movement across borders is a big challenge in itself in addition to the security nightmares. GDPR, for example, does not allow PII movement outside EU borders; there are other challenges with data from US especially defense data or financial data. Few startups consider security and privacy collectively, which is fine initially, however, adequate important should be given to each of these topics and it would make sense to consult the experts in these areas because no matter how beautiful, user-friendly and great UI the product may have, it will fail the interest of markets, especially investors when it comes to security and privacy.
4. Think lean: The technology operations costs are high for any business and startups are no exceptions. The initial technology ideas that might flow in bringing life into the product can be so overwhelming that the later operations and maintenance costs might take a hike initially. Make no mistakes here because ultimately, a startup might get into a situation of keep-or-throw position for certain technology pieces where both options cost them dearly.
5. Virtual and remote working: It is relatively easier for technology companies to have part of their teams work remotely or virtually. And

when it comes to COVID-19 like situations (yes, it is not an everyday phenomenon but it is here), the startups that can continue working from remote locations or virtually will remain in the race.

These situations decide the survivor while many startups will close shops, the one who can endure a pandemic through working collaboratively, from remote as a virtual team will come out successful.

title:
Is it Cost or Speed - Either way, You Pay !

Nagraj N
Sr. HR Director | Board Director | Delivery Head | People & Culture | M&A |
Capability Builder | Change Leader

An architect behind 5 successful Tech. start-ups - Built & led the People Function, while scaling from 1 to 30+ countries, from 5 to 4000+ employees, from a few thousands to millions of users, from $0 to $100M+ ARR (annual recurring revenue), from the basement to $500M+ valuation & further, to successful exits. A successful HR leader with strong business experience as a Board Director, as a Delivery Head, regular customer connects & an inherent belief in culture & people, helps me to create and implement, business specific tailored strategies, that drives talent to deliver extraordinary business value.

https://www.linkedin.com/in/nagarajn4457621/

One of my connections on LinkedIn viewed my profile & asked me, **"You say you have been with 5 successful start-ups, what's the secret sauce for a successful startup"**? Even after 5 start-ups, scaling them across the globe... real successful ones too, the answer eluded me. If I really have to nail it down, I'd say it's **"Time"**.

The most important thing the founder/CEO has is "Time".

You somehow have to create more time within the day, if the value & the business has to grow. Easy to say, but how?

First, Get the right people and position them where **They Can Do What You Do & More**.

Deploy them in such roles where they can have the maximum impact & this frees up your first chunk of **"Time"**.

Every start-up faces the same set of challenges & compete in the same markets. But only a few emerge successful. Talent is available. But not having the right tools/ person, can hamper your ability to effectively attract & engage the talent needed to fill these roles quickly at scale. In the beginning, the founder is directly involved in every hiring decision. You have to be, as you would want to hire those, who can move the organization forward. The aim is to get people who want to change the world & many times, better & faster than the founders. Are you seeing the speed & what it can achieve in terms of **"Time"**?

After the first 50 hires typically, it becomes unmanageable so the managers take up the task of hiring. If you aren't careful, there's a tendency to lower the bar. The reasons can be many but often, the managers could be looking out for themselves. High potentials can be seen as a threat & avoided. It's not that smart people dropped. It's just that, the preference leans towards those who are not smarter than them. Over time, when amplified, what do you think would happen? The journey down this path & the correction(s) are a sheer waste of time, effort & money to the company... But what hits you hard is the lost "Time".

It's for the founder & the CHRO to get the culture right, to build & hold firmly, the talent systems and culture necessary for linking talent to value.

Here's where micromanagement is important - **Micromanage the process, it's needed, but never the people**. The measure of a good hire is the speed at which they are able to get on to the job, once they come on board. More the time they take, evaluate the hiring process.

Attracting talent is a sheer marketing & branding exercise. Couple it with a clear vision & candidates / employees will identify with it and dream along with the founders. It fuels the cells, to be a part of something incredible, something bigger than their daily routine.

A good story has a way to inspire, never forget that. An uninspiring vision or lack of vision or failing to communicate in spite of a clear vision - just makes your struggle for talent all the more harder & longer. You lose **"Time"**.

Now that you have got the people in, **have you thought of middle management**? A balance needs to be achieved - It's good to encourage employees to take the initiative. As employees grow, learn within the company, the more invested they are in your business. By giving a chance to strive for a higher position, you'll reduce training time.

It's also important to recognize that middle management plays a very important role : As they lead your teams, they bridge the gap between you and your employees. They are to execute everything as intended. That's a major reason for them to be superbly good at what they do. It's not easy & not everyone can manage big teams. It's better to consider someone seasoned, who has done it before with a proven track record of success. It saves **"Time"**.

Second, Use the freed-up time in molding - As Jack Welch said, *"My main job was developing talent. I was a gardener providing water & other nourishment to our top people. Of course, I had to pull out some weeds too"*.

Hold yourself & your team accountable. Lack of accountability slowly rots the organization from inside. Not everyone is fully owning a function or project, your employees might not feel responsible the way you do. Give feedback. It's about you as a leader - the daily interactions that result in small adjustments of employee performance and behavior. If someone is deviating from the path, it's stupid to let him continue the same way for a year, or a quarter or even a week without saying anything. Immediate feedback & guidance on their performance benefits everyone & saves **"Time"**.

Don't take too long to weed out those people you think, can't contribute or aren't up to the job.

You & your CHRO need to identify & **have a deep understanding of your top talent, the critical 2%**. Never make the mistake of thinking that these are people in the top management. This talent when deployed has a disproportionate return on investment. Know them, understand them, else you cannot deploy them effectively. Give them roles where they can create significant value as they are your most vital people. The ability to deploy and redeploy talent, as opportunities come & go, can be your key differentiator from your competitor - Once again, are you ready in **"Time"**?

Third, Plan six months to 1 year ahead of time. Identify specifically those things that you would no longer do - the things you can pass on to others. Decide who would take them over and how you need to get each person ready for that role. It's not processes, organization, or money - **Your highest leverage is your people**.

Your organization's overall performance can be measured by just 3 points: Employee Engagement, Customer Satisfaction (including innovation), and Cash-flow. And employee engagement demands your **"TIME"**, because remember, the market will continue to say **"Make something people want"** but don't forget, it also includes '**making a company that people want to work for**'.

Sailing on The Winds of Organizational Culture

I read a quote today - Growing a culture requires a good storyteller. Changing a culture requires a persuasive editor. I had seen it done in one of my early stints... Further, had attempted it. Failed at it badly. But Failures, a true friend, teaches you more than success ever can. Attempted again with a lot more deliberation & over a period of time, my learning has only increased voraciously.

Having met success a few times & failure ever willing to dance with me, just waiting for that little slip, have I been able to nail down on an absolute model to build an organization culture? No! Definitely not! It is fluid by nature. A few guidelines are what I have, to raise the sail & catch the wind...

Let's get sailing - Ahoy!!

We need to know where we are sailing to - We need to visualize it

It takes time, effort, and commitment to build the desired culture in any company. If I don & have these three to give, I cannot stop from a culture being built. It just might not be the desired one. But it begins with the leaders of the company developing a strategic vision & backing it up with clear, visible changes in behaviour. As the quote said, you need a good storyteller, and a good story too.

But it's the persuasive editor who would craft a great change story, that helps leaders communicate the need for change to the rest of the company.

Let's lift the sail – It's action time

Small focus groups with trained leaders are brought together at this point as priorities are to be defined, right practices are to be chosen, detailed initiatives are to be designed and proposed - to ensure that there is a clear link to the desired broader transformation.

Effective communication, the key to share the new vision clearly with the staff.

Leaders & supervisors are given extensive training on this. But it's important that the company's vision & the employee's needs are aligned. Managers at this point are to explain to their teams how their individual roles contribute to the company's strategic goals & how important it is. Time to set examples, time for praises to reinforce effective behaviors. Managers trained in coaching and mentoring techniques, provide on-the-spot pats or development advice to their team. Many formal & informal ways are adopted to celebrate employee achievements.

Leaders are to focus on the importance of KPIs, discuss & explain at regular staff meetings on exactly how the performance of each specific unit impacts on the financial, operational success of the company as a whole.

Best Talent Practices For Startups

Daya Prakash

Entrepreneur | Founder - TalentOnLease | Providing World Class IT Talent | Ex-CIO, LG | CXO-Intellect

I have been in the enterprise and digital technology domains for a little over two decades and have vast experience at a global level.Before starting my entrepreneurial journey as Founder www.TalentOnLease.com which is into providing "IT Talent On Demand", I served LG India as the CIO (Chief Information Officer).My stint at LG between 2001 and 2013 helped me transform from a mere IT Leader to an evolved and matured Business Leader with in-depth knowledge on various aspects of Management of Business, leveraging the power of IT both at strategic and tactical levels.My contribution at LG not only fetched me recognition internally but also in the industry by way of winning several prestigious awards and accolades for the path-breaking work I'd done over the years. The credit for this exceptional growth solely goes to LG which grew from a few millions to a whopping 3.5 Billion USD during my tenure with it.

https://www.linkedin.com/in/dayaprakash/

The Premise

Various studies conducted in the past few years have established and reiterated the fact that the biggest challenge faced by the start-up is finding the right talent. Unless the start-up has been able to establish itself as an aspirational brand or have backing of some of the biggest VC funds, allowing you to assume the position of extravagant in talent acquisition. There is perpetual war for talent and attracting right talent isn't easy.

Wouldn't it be fabulous if a start-up could hire the most suitable candidate without having to spend days and days interviewing lots of prospective employees?

Startups spend a lot of time and money on interviewing candidates. If none of them are suitable, then they have to start the process all over again. If a start-up is fortunate in finding the right candidate then also they have to wait for the candidate to join until the candidate joins them, the challenges of hiring are not over for them.

Here are the top reasons start-ups are struggling to hire suitable candidates –

1. Competition from other employers – Employer Branding
2. The low shelf life of Top Talent
3. Ability to reach Passive Job Seekers
4. Candidates don't have the right skills (technical, domain and soft skills)

So how does a start-up evaluate what's working for them and what's not?

Recruiting metrics are the key to assessing the robustness and effectiveness of a start-up's recruiting process. It is incredibly vital to have measurable goals and data to track the performance.

This shows where you stand as a company, particularly when you're trying to make game- changing hires. Recruiting metrics enable you to understand where you should be allocating your time and budget.

Let's take a look at some critical hiring ratios and learn the best ways to measure them:

1. Cost Per Hire
2. Cost per hire estimates the average cost incurred by a company on filling an opening from sourcing to on-boarding. It can either make or break the yearly budget of a company.
3. Time To Fill
4. Time to fill shows your hiring speed, and it boils down to how long a recruiter takes to fill an opening from the time of a listed vacancy. It is the total number of days taken from advertising a job opening to bringing a candidate on-board. It exhibits the productivity of the recruiter and the efficiency of the recruitment process.

Quality Of Hires

The quality of hire metric reflects the performance of the hiring team in terms of the quality of faithful candidates. It is the difference between several candidates and top choice candidates. It gives an idea to the company of whether recruiters are squandering their time and effort in search of top talent or making maximum utilization of available resources.

A Reality Check

Once an organization has the key matrices defined to measure the performance they should study the Conversion Rate. Conversion rate is the direct correlation between the number of candidates who were shortlisted in screening for further processing to the ones who accepted the offer and joined.

A complete analysis of what is working out and what's not working out based on the conversion rate should be carried out. It would be wise to analyse the source of prospective employees to make decisions about future investments into right channels. The source of hire captures where most of your new employees come from, whether it is job boards, agencies, professional/social networks, or employee referrals.

The Suggested Approach

1. Data-Driven Hiring
2. The moment we talk about measuring something, it's evident that data is involved. When it comes to measuring, data is vital. Once you gather all the data of your company, pick the most startling numbers and look for ways to improve them. Following a data-driven approach to hiring will give you access to some of the top talents in various industries.
3. AI/ML Based Screening
4. A data-driven approach leads to the use of data in the right way. Using IT systems that can pull raw data using AI and machine learning consistently and retain every data point is essential to improve the hiring ratio. AI/ML

enables you to be more informed at what you do by compiling the correct data while helping you effectively sift through loads of data.

Application Tracking System

An excellent application tracking system helps you at every point of your hiring process. It begins from posting your job ad to notifying you in real- time as people apply to the entire journey of hiring.

Assessments

Companies should use tools to assess the candidates on given skills.

There are several tools available today to perform this effectively where one could assess technical, logical & reasoning and coding skills before proceeding for an interview to avoid time and money wastage.

Video Interviews

Lags in scheduling interviews add to your time to hire. Conducting multiple rounds of interviews kills a lot of time and consists of a lot of room for improvement. There are technologies available today for conducting video interviews which will help you screen the initial phase, which reduces your time drastically to hire and close the selection process.

Conclusion

Effective utilization of technologies and Forecasting Your Hiring needs well would certainly help you triumph. An internal database of previously rejected candidates or a group of candidates you've pre-screened for specific roles helps you reduce your time to hire.I would like to conclude it with a simple advice that when you deal with challenge of improving hiring ratio be cautious about

1. Cost of hiring
2. Cost of wrong hiring

As startups end up spending huge money and also waste a lot of time for each of the wrong hires.

MVP Approach for Startups During and Post Covid-19

S. Koushik Debroy
Co-Founder & CPO, TheCodeWork

Ashish Singh
Co-Founder & CEO, TheCodeWork

Ashish and I (Koushik) have been friends from our engineering days. Both of us were always passionate about building products right from our college days and started our careers with different startups to learn the nuances of the industry. After a few years of working at different startups, we decided to start our own venture with an HealthTech Product, "VizitDoc", which bridges down the gap between rural and urban healthcare. It was after the development of the product we realized the market needs of MVP Development and thus we ventured our MVP-First Product Development Company, "TheCodeWork".

https://www.linkedin.com/in/s-koushik-debroy-02349155
https://www.linkedin.com/in/imrealashu

https://thecodework.com/blog/what-every-entrepreneur-should-know-about-building-an-mvp

Minimum Viable Product (MVP) offers a unique development tool where a new idea is validated within the markets before scaling up or even developing the entire product with the wings of its utility features.While the market might have presented with different opportunities, but with the looming global economic crisis due to COVID-19, it's absolutely essential for every entrepreneur to utilize their resources very wisely while chasing their dreams.

Key Factors for a new venture during Covid-19

With the exponential growth of COVID-19 cases, a global lockdown has been enforced. It has impacted small businesses tremendously where the demand has dipped over the months. In these testing times lookout for these factors while starting out a new venture.

● Industry: Industry is one of the key factors to look out for during this crisis as some industries like healthcare have bloomed during this time while others like travel & tourism have gone downhill. If your product can serve multiple industries, it is always essential to target a niche first before scaling wide. With the opportunities presented, it will be foolish to target all lucrative industries right at the beginning as it will make you lose your focus and reduce the credibility of a niche target market.

● Demand and Competitors: Every industry has multiple players but the leaning of the consumer demand towards a specific brand is transparent. Analyzing and releasing your product with MVP gives you the ability to quickly identify the need of the hour that influences the demand. The sudden shock of a pandemic has made it the epicenter of all consumer demands which means consumers are now spending more or less on products that have a direct/indirect impact of COVID-19.

● Platform: Choosing your platform of release and branding has never been as critical as that during the pandemic. With the extended lockdown, the work from home culture is dominant, and consumers are switching their mode of interaction with different platforms. Even though there is an upsurge in user engagement of social media channels, consumers are spending less time on a single post with multiple options available. Initially, finding the right fit to get product feedback is crucial. Moreover, the strategy to go mobile-only may not be the best idea right away as consumers tend to spend more time with friends and family, personal devices like cell phones get sidelined. The strategy with the MVP is to find the right fit to get feedback during the initial release.

● Cost: This is the most crucial factor during the pandemic. As an entrepreneur, it has become almost essential to validate your business idea with your bootstrap money before raising capital funds. Of course, entrepreneurs are raising funds during their ideation phase as well but genuine traction helps the case more often.

COVID-19 has created havoc in the employment sector as it has become more vulnerable with people losing their jobs. Spending on product development and other key essentials for the company needs to be well thought out even with the capital funds.

Taking the MVP approach towards product development helps you minimize the cost by focusing only on the core essentials.

• Time: Another important factor to focus on during and after the crisis, is the essence of time. The urgency of certain products within the market is evident but ignoring the user feedback and building products with false assumptions will only waste your valuable time and money. Instead, the lean strategy with an MVP approach will help you validate your idea, faster, and help reach your product-market fit in quick successions. With the hope of getting into our new normal, being a front runner within a niche will increase brand credibility. Making precise and early releases is the way to lead forward.

The MVP Program by TheCodeWork is precisely built for entrepreneurs willing to apply the strategy for product development. With our MVP program, we are helping them develop their products with a go-to-market strategy. Global changes are evident for the pandemic and it is almost permanent. As an entrepreneur, it is the challenge we thrive upon to turn the situation to our benefit by making smart moves.

Synopsis

MVP or Minimum Viable Product is a concept much popularised by Eric Ries who laid the lean strategy for startups and other organizations alike. Characteristically it is used to generate enough evidence and test out the core idea before shipping the entire product. With the pandemic outbreak, it has become crucial for the entrepreneurs to make the most of the resources that they have in hand and MVP is the way to it.The fundamentals of MVP during COVID-19 crisis include grasping the niche market before producing a multiservice provider, understanding and comprehending a valid consumer preference and value, choosing the proper platform for product launch, minimizing the cost of product development and using the best of resources via the MVP approach to save time and use it judiciously.

Dr. Satheesh Kumar Reddy Chinnapapagari

Entrepreneur and Start-up mentor

Dr. Satheesh is a visionary leader with proven international success in edtech, medtech and healthcare space, building products and providing leadership in unique challenging markets to quickly analyse key business drivers and develop growth strategies. He strongly believes that it takes the right combination of people, process, technology, data and timing to build the best solutions. He has several credible international recognitions as a Top 100 EdTech leader and Top 20 Indian CEOs in the Start-ups founded in the U.S.

https://in.linkedin.com/in/drsatheeshkumarreddyc

The value lies in what gets used, not in what gets built – Kris Gal

The current COVID19 control health measures have led to significant behavioural shifts and economic disruption, creating a fairly unpredictable system. This crisis driven fundamental change in consumer behaviour is already driving significant online adoption across groceries, general commerce, gaming, education and healthcare. During and post-covid19 economic downturn, consumer demand for "nice-to-have" products goes down as buyers focus more on their basic needs. Health, wellness and safety products that fit into the lower parts of "Maslow's Hierarchy of Needs" become the top priority.

Hence, the impact of COVID-19 will usher a new paradigm in how brands think about product launches. It is during such times a paradigm shift happens, reshaping the entire product launch landscape.

New product launches during and post COVID19 are going to be game changing moments for any business because of accelerated customer acquisition favouring certain products and brands over others. While the edtech, and healthtech businesses are already racing on this opportunity, there is a huge opening in the health, hygiene and immunity space for new product launches as covid19 has posed a complete change in the consumer and customer experiences.

New product launch is like harvesting, where all your efforts culminate and get realized, hence you need to ensure a successful launch with four main ingredients - online presence, right messaging, empathy, social responsibility and key partnerships in solving the crisis.

"The new normal for any new product launch, is how to get the customers online ensuring best data privacy practices."

Also, customers will remember empathy during and long after the COVID19 crisis has passed, hence any business would have to raise their bar on empathy. The brands that genuinely care about their base, and about humanity in general will need to get their messaging right for the new product launches and show their contributions towards solving the problems customers are grappling with right now and offer certain portions of the profits spent on organizations to help solve the COVID-19 crisis.

In today's crisis situation, the early ones to race ahead will be the ones who can identify and work with partners, as this can be a powerful source of competitive advantage for creating new growth products or solutions and business models. During crisis and economic downturns, it is the partnerships that can get you speed to market and get you the biggest scale and the biggest returns.

Pre-selling your product is an ideal way to ensure the pump is primed before you even start building your product. The many advantages of pre-selling your product idea is that you will receive validation of the market demand and the viability of your pricing model. Also, it is a great way to reduce the risk inherent with a new product build as you are establishing demand, and a ready market for it through customer partnerships.

The threat of COVID-19 has thrown the sales and marketing domains completely into turmoil, bringing in a paradigm shift towards a virtual future through virtual trade shows, showcase webinars and special events. Businesses will adapt to either a complete virtual approach or a blended approach with both traditional trade shows and *virtual trade shows* to cut down costs and time. Some companies might favour *showcase webinars* such as online meetings and presentations, by inviting journalists, consumers, and industry insiders to discuss and market their products in a more low-key manner.

Also through *"special events"* vendors can host their own product launch and announcement events for industry insiders, journalists and stream such events online to reach a broader worldwide audience with a more comprehensive and exhaustive approach.

These three new trends, virtual launches, showcase webinars and special events will bring in the concept of *varied release schedules* which will help empower brands to create their own timelines and release products at any right time. Such launches can be done when a new product is most needed, or at a time when the brand doesn't have to compete with industry heavy weights for media share.

Brands will start to engage into more *sustained marketing initiatives* like spreading their budget across timeframes. Shrinking marketing budgets and tight timelines will definitely encourage a virtual future as saving on both money and time are relevant and significant. Brands with major international trade show schedules, are also faced with the challenge of targeting every corner of the globe at once.

However, the new paradigm will lead to *increased regionalism* through *localized marketing*, where launches target different regions, possibly even on varying release dates. Moving forward, self-hosted and localized launches will allow brands to more accurately gauge demand and make necessary adjustments before unveiling into other geographies.

This shift in new product release strategies will not put an end to the traditional methods but will drive the trend towards a more virtual, fragmented landscape which will give brands the ability to adopt their schedules to when the market opportunity is greatest.

The new product launching companies need to understand the emotional, psychological, and economic drivers, the "why" behind behavioural changes; what those changes look like; and how, going forward, they will impact consumer purchase behaviour. This may require facing the fact that our current definition of innovation, at least as it applies to products, needs to be radically revised.

Synopsis in 5 Points.

1. Digital first, is the new normal during and post-COVID19 for any new product launch. Hence businesses need to accelerate their online presence and focus on digital, technology and analytics ensuring best privacy and security practices.
2. Pre-selling the new product idea even before a launch to ensure a right product market fit, validating pricing models, establishing customer partnerships will rise and become the next norm.
3. Taking social responsibility during crisis businesses can raise the bar on empathy can scale the new product experience into a social experience.
4. Marketing will see a paradigm shift towards a blended or a virtual future rather than the traditional trade shows. Virtual trade shows, showcase webinars and special events will be the new product launch trends.
5. We will start seeing more adaptive ecosystems where businesses will require new partnerships and non-traditional collaborations, including strategic M&A.

The Mistakes and opportunities of first time startups and entrepreneurs – A Lubricant Startup Experience

Dr Holger Streetz
Director of Business Development @ Bathan AG, Switzerland.

Holger studied economics in Germany and the Czech Republic and holds a doctor in law. He has 10 years of experience in working for a niche high performance lubricant supplier with a strong focus on biomass and other renewable energies. Holger is a well-respected speaker at international conferences and is regularly contributing to professional journals such as the Pellet Mill Magazine. He is passionate about the project Power2Crypto – the leading Integrated Energy 2.0 technology – converting renewable energy that cannot be fed in the grid into crypto currencies.

https://www.linkedin.com/in/dr-holger-streetz

Entering a market as a startup is exciting! So many opportunities and so much to do. You have an excellent product that outperforms the standard products in your target markets and are enthusiastic about sharing your news with potential customers. Often the expectation is that changing to a better product is obvious and changeover time should be brief. The business plan reflects these assumptions accordingly.

B2B markets are very different from B2C markets

However, there are some Do's and Don'ts that have to be kept in mind. B2B market, you go up against companies with deep pockets, well-equipped R&D departments, established relationships with customers, and a well-known brand. Advertising concepts such as with B2C industries do not always apply for B2B markets. Additionally, it is not so easy to recognize whom to talk with. A top-down approach might end up being stuck with middle management or operators.

Especially with technical products and applications, CEOs rely on the expertise of their engineers and operators rather than the promises of a sales representative of a company he has never heard of before. If you have convinced the operators and plant managers of your products and services, the bottom-up approach might get stuck with the purchasing department or top management, refusing to try out products and services they cannot assess the risk for.

Therefore, keep in mind that

1. Convince all parties involved in the decision process
2. Make sure to emphasize your reliability and make the decision makers feel comfortable about your offerings
3. Be supportive in terms of sharing your expertise, explaining the advantages from the right angle depending on who you talk to, and position yourself as a solution provider rather than a supplier.

In B2B industries, decision makers are not always and only looking for the cheapest product or service, but for a long-term solution to their problems. The investments in equipment are immense and the opportunity costs of down time a constant risk to profitability. This makes it even harder for startups to enter such markets, because potential customers tend to be risk averse.

In the wind power industry for example, the investment strategy spans some 20 years. A cement plant might never change large equipment in 50 years, as seen in former GDR cement plants. The equipment was planned oversized to reduce wear to a minimum, thus lasting forever.

Having a good product is not everything

Assumed, the product is great and has the potential to be disruptive and game changing. There are still hurdles to overcome to be really market ready. The costs and time involved in completing formal requirements for complying with industry standards are often underestimated. In the case of lubricants, this involves but is not limited to tests for all technical data, certifications for OEM approval, engine bench tests, gear bench tests, field tests, and other certifications e.g. for food safety, Halal, Kosher, and customer specific requirements.

Most of these tasks have to be completed by third parties involving high costs and plenty of time.

How to address B2B markets in the social media era

The resources in startups are limited and have to be spent wisely. If a product or service is applicable with more than one industry, you should focus on one or two industries before aiming to gain traction in all of them at the same time. Networking – attending conferences, trade shows and industry meetings, actively taking part in industry associations, visiting potential customers, social media – is expensive and time consuming. However, it is a necessary task to get your brand out to the audience.

Conferences are a great tool to present innovations and new products and services to a specific audience. Sponsoring the event improves your attention and gives you the opportunity to explain in one-on-one meetings. Industry associations are a great tool to receive first-hand information and to get in touch with potential customers and decision makers in a relaxed environment. It will take some time to be "accepted" by the club, but worth the efforts.

Social Selling in B2B marketing is not very popular yet. However, it is becoming more and more important in building strong customer relations, generating qualified leads and outperforming established sales pitches. Social selling means highlighting yourself as a thought-leader and industry professional (B2B-influencer and Topics Ambassador) to a target audience. Buyers are far more likely to engage with sales professionals, if they are known for their high-quality contributions to the industry.

This opportunity eventually increases momentum. The person has to be venturesome to stage her professional self and willing to invest in building credibility. This is a constant process rather than a one-time investment. It pays off in being known as a professional expert and B2B-influencer rather than a salesperson.

Variance is a constant companion

In the early stages and later on, growth has a high variance. Do not expect your business to monthly grow, but accept the industry specific cycles. Setbacks in growth are natural and depend on many factors, such as holidays and annual accounts season or budget planning. This is nothing to be afraid of. However, if the competition is being alert or other suppliers deliver faulty products causing problems with your customer, you have to analyze the situation in close cooperation with your customer, making sure you support her and emphasizing it is not your product that caused the downtime. The small company is always the weakest link in the chain of suppliers and the easiest to replace.

Find strength in the niche

The goal is to strengthen your position from the weakest chain link to a partner your customer's trust. This requires strong expertise, a good customer support, deep knowledge of the industry and a product or service that is able to outperform the competition. Reaching this position in a niche market is relatively easy, because of the small number of players, products and services.

My company struggled some time finding a market that is offering the quantities and accessibility needed to gain traction. We focused on the biomass and wind power sector. Pelleting wood is relatively simple, comparable to making pasta. However, the consumption of lubricants was high and the existing products were of low quality. Our ceramic lubricants were able to outperform the standard products by reducing grease consumption by 95% and prolonging the lifetime of bearings by up to factor 10.

With this advantage, we were able to convince risk averse plant managers to switch lubricants. We hired two engineers with combined 30 years of experience in commissioning, servicing and repairing pellet plants, so we had the knowledge, a network with operators and plant managers and were outperforming the competition. With the strong position in one niche market, we had the financial strength to expand into other niche markets, such as wind power, cement and rail. From the experience gained in wood pelleting and developing a new food grade grease we easily entered the market for animal feed.

The takeaway from these short insights into a startup lubricant supplier shows that there can be bureaucratic hurdles to overcome and industry standards to comply. Sometimes, it is very expensive and time consuming. Investors in startups demand constant improvement in sales and internal processes, but setbacks are natural. As long as they are due to industry specific fluctuations and not due to actions by the competition. As a startup with a product that is applicable with many industries, it is wise to find a niche, grow steadily, and build expertise rather than juggling too many balls at once.

Do not underestimate the power of Social Selling in B2B marketing. Especially startups can benefit from positioning individuals as B2B-influencers and thought leaders.

AI In Transport & Logistics Industry

Ese-Osarumen H. Efesomwan
Managing Director at Business Brokerage And
Investment Company PTY Ltd - BBIC

Firstly, I want to say an excessively big thank you to Ravi Kikan for giving me this great opportunity to express myself in such a large audience. You are doing a wonderful job for the Tech Start-up community.

We all understand that artificial intelligence (AI) in a very substantial way has changed the nature of services amidst the global pandemic, there has been improved and more organized methods of operations in all aspects of life leaving no sector untouched. My name is Ese-Osarumen H.O Efesomwan, I am the President, a Researcher and Product Development specialist for the tech startup BBIC Technology Corporation; an Organization with a C-Corp Incorporation.

This Topic given to me is in line with an ongoing Research project (ILP 1.0) in my company. Now, I will pick a case study using an industry which I am currently Researching on; (The transportation and logistics industry).

AI will help to maximize productivity rate, customer satisfaction, efficiency and facilitate cost effectiveness. My current project center's on global unemployment and logistics operation solutions amidst the global pandemic.

From my Research I realized that it is possible to run logistic operations with increased cost effectiveness and at the same time create jobs for the global unemployed society. This is what we are researching on BBIC and we have just concluded the BBIC ILP 1.0 phase... We have ILP programs in three (3) phases. We're currently working on a mind mirroring program, biometrics, IOTs, Emotional intelligence and Human Technology; we believe if devices can connect and communicate at a certain frequency humans can too. For more conversations, if you would like to be a part of my Research team, corporate sponsorship of the BBIC Technology Corporation is open and fully operational with authorized shares and membership certificates.

"There is no limit to what the human mind can do, if you hear the Whispers then you're talented like myself and know you can do anything you put your mind to," AS FAR AS YOUR EYES CAN SEE"

Synopsis

1. Artificial Intelligence will bring orderliness in the New world.
2. You all should watch out for advanced biometrics systems
3. An individual who uses AI for productivity is accurately more efficient than the other who is not.

The Secret Sauce for a 10X Sustainable Growth

Nitten Bhinhhani
Enabling Early-stage Startups to be Investor-Ready

- Enabling Early-stage Startups to be Investors-Ready.
- Creator of Awesome Pitch Decks that help you get Funded, Fast!
- 10X Sustainable Growth Enabler through Customer Experience.

https://www.linkedin.com/in/nittenbz

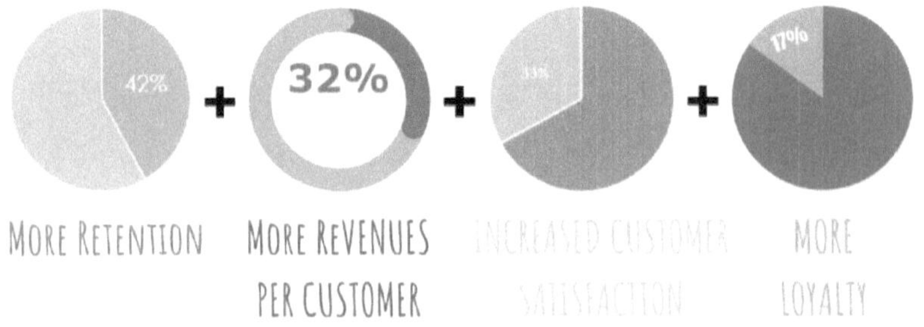

There have been scores of examples, where the startups used (or continue to use) the deep discounts strategy to gain 4X customers, whether it's due to the investors' pressure or the founders are too focussed on the valuation, is altogether a different question.

Of course, these startups gain those 4X customers, but at what costs ?

Eventually, their existing infrastructure just can't cope up when it's confronted with the enormous teething troubles, which they hadn't been prepared for in the first place. As a result, the profitable customers who are now frustrated for being ignored (even once), just switch to the competition.

These startups are now left with almost all loss-making customers who only transact, till the time discounts are offered.

The outcome of this deep discount strategy leads to any or all of the below impacts:

1. Running Out of Cash (top 2nd reason, "Why Startups Fail"): Deep discounting is the fastest way to "run out of cash" i.e. losing Rs.1 / Rs.2 on the transaction value of Rs.4 is a sure-shot way to burn out!
2. Getting Outcompeted (top 4th reason, "Why Startups Fail"): Your profitable customers switch to competition because you no longer care for them as your whole focus is now on getting new customers onboard. Not only do they switch to competition, but they also share their bad experiences with their family, friends, and social media too (70% buying still depends on Positive Word of Mouth). It's now 6-7 times more costly for such startups, to get a new customer!
3. Pricing/Cost Issues (top 5th reason, "Why Startups Fail"): Same as "Running Out of Cash" i.e. losing Rs.1 / Rs.2 to show the transaction value of Rs.4
4. Ignoring (Existing) Customers (top 9th reason, "Why Startups Fail"): Same as "Getting Outcompeted" i.e. Your existing customers not only leave you but also rant against you with their family, friends and on social media.
5. Both the founders and the investors have thus realized that the startups shouldn't just satisfy but delight their customers, and should simultaneously focus on the profitable and sustainable growth path.

A "Satisfied Customer" is the best strategy of all. Indeed, every company's greatest assets are its Customers"

Michael Leboeuf, American Business Author & Management Professor

So, what's the secret to a 10X sustainable growth even in tough times?

Delighted, Loyal Customers! Yes, you read it right.

Take a look at benefits offered by Customer Experience **(CX)**:

- 42% more retention i.e. better revenues
- 32% more revenues per customer i.e. higher revenue growth & gross margins
- 33% increased customer satisfaction i.e. more happy customers, who bring in additional qualified leads for you
- 17%+ more loyalty i.e. each loyal customer = 10X their first purchase
- 66% probability to up-sell / resell to existing customers
- 15%+ operational savings in serving the existing customers
- Why is Customer Experience (CX) a must for Star**tups and MSMEs** ?

   As today's most powerful competitive differentiation, "Customer Experience Strategy" empowers any business to easily disrupt even the most crowded industry, maximize its success, and create a sustainable 10X growth path in the long-term.

How Artificial Intelligence will change the nature of services During and Post COVID-19 ?

Bandinee Pradhan

Entrepreneur | Research Enthusiast | Case Study Author

Bandinee is the founder of a technology company focusing on solving complex business problems and helping organizations using data science and artificial intelligence. She is a marketing research enthusiast and has published business case studies about digital services and business growth.

https://www.linkedin.com/in/bandinee-pradhan-69295166

In a short period of time, COVID-19 has overwhelmed lives and livelihoods around the globe. Industries are working speedily to transit to this "new normal" phase.

Artificial Intelligence (AI) has been in headlines for a few years and seems to be moving from "idea" to "action". Hence, it is important to discuss how AI is being used during COVID-19 and what will change post-COVID-19.

During COVID 19

Healthcare Services: The fundamental health is of utmost importance now given how pre- existing conditions are thought to be worsening the COVID-19 effect. One of the basic symptoms of the coronavirus is "fever". Devices like thermometers or other temperature measurement equipment are being connected to the cloud and into a database and using AI- based models to analyse it, authorities worldwide are mapping the real-time situation i.e. cluster or hotspot where body temperature is spiking. The same is applicable for wearables health devices.

Health tracking devices are notifying individuals and healthcare professionals about any abnormality such as body temperature and heart rate. In addition to potentially tracking and predicting the spread of COVID-19, experts are developing AI models to use in the diagnosis and prognosis of the disease. In fact, this is perhaps where most of the first rush of AI initiatives focused on. Fast and accurate diagnosis of COVID-19 can save lives, limit the spread of the disease, and generate data on which to train AI models. There is a growing effort to train AI models to diagnose COVID-19 using chest radiography images.

A recent review by Bullock et al. (2020) suggests how AI can save the time of the healthcare professional by performing a faster and accurate diagnosis.

Robots and Drones: Robots and drones are being used to deliver medical supplies, monitor public gatherings, in some cases, they are also being used to disinfect public areas. These robots and drones are using AI to identify the places and people.

Customer Services: COVID-19 pandemic has made it clear to brands that customer insights are the key priorities. AI can help in matching demand and supply. The surge of unstructured data can be analysed using AI to ensure that production and supply are optimized. Brands are focusing on essential products as it can be seen how they are trying to fulfil the demand for Personal Protection Equipment (PPE). Another trend seen in retail was adopting a faster online channel of delivery of products. AI-enabled chatbots are being used to manage orders and delivery of products. Similarly, for banking services AI is being used to identify and verify documents as most of the work is being done remotely.

Post COVID19

A paradigm shift is going to happen in the form of accelerated AI adoption in goods and services. A glimpse of Industry 4.0 or the AI-era has already witnessed the growing cloud computing and big data. However, post COVID19 the new normal of social distancing will make the AI-driven economy a reality. The increasing use of AI, machine learning, cloud computing, big data, and automation are bridging the gap between machines and humans.

The following are the goals likely to be achieved in the Industry 4.0 era.

- Higher automation
- More digital led-businesses
- More information and communications strategies

Since, social distancing and preventive measures have made it difficult for customers to do activities like walking to the grocery store, dining out with friends and family. The demand patterns are shifting hence, digital-led businesses will continue to grow and companies adapting to this by innovating product or delivery models will establish a strong brand image. AI is expected to grow by $14.05 billion in 2023 in the retail industry. AI and ML will play a vital role in redefining communication solutions. The AI/ML system will continuously monitor the situation and help to make decisions related or purchase delivery of products or services. This will enhance the user experience.

"Nothing in life is to be feared, it is only to be understood. Now is the time to understand more, so that we may fear less."
— Marie Curie.

Synopsis :

1. Use of AI will accelerate post COVID19
2. AI can help humans save time
3. Industry 4.0 will see more innovative products and ideas
4. AI will help humans fight COVID-19: from identification to delivering medicines
5. Adoption of digital channels/businesses will increase as social distancing will be the new normal

Productivity Tracking For Startups During & Post Covid 19

Raghav Belavadi

Founder & CEO - Hype Luxury Mobility

A serial entrepreneur and a fromer global leader from accenture. Founded Hype in India to begin the new cult of luxury mobility among the millennials and executives. An innovation specialist and overt speaker who is a staunch follower of Steve Jobs and grooming himself to be the Iron Man of India ;)

https://www.linkedin.com/in/raghavbelavadi

Creating something is easier, Execution is the hard part but, maintaining that is the hardest of all. Best companies have always found out creative ways to ensure they track and monitor their work.

Over the years I have understood and come to firmly believe that traction is the most critical part of business becoming success.Be it Product or marketing or Sales or Operations, tracking your productivity throughout matters the most. For every dollar spent on any of the tasks, it must pay for itself as an ROI and this needs to be revealed to the team. A/B testing is best across all verticals of a startup to see what is working and what is not.

Traction again helps in knitting all pieces of work together from Marketing, Sales and Operations and feeds into Product and services as an essential element to fuel growth. What customers are liking and what is working as desired exactly leads us to the right Target Audience (Target group).

Let me give you an example of what we did in my startup. Our target audience is a premium customer group. When we did the segmentation of the customer base we realised that the top 20% of the customer base is naturally driven to our services and once we acquire them we just need to engage them as they are often loyal to the brand.

About 60% of the community was at a tipping point for a change over and needed to ensure reinforced brand recall and higher levels of engagement. The remaining section was an endeavour to increase visibility and probably never a customer base.

When we started to track our productivity we got all the essential details like customer satisfaction index, pain points, user experience, engagement ratio etc. We used these vitals to alter our work in every area of customer engagement to see success.

Again success is just a journey and this constantly evolves to be kept a tight watch upon.

Productivity is not just releasing tons of features in a product or a series of service offerings or bombarding the digital media with creatives. Remember, more features and lesser utilisation is a spoiler of your key metrics too. Achieving the optimal balance between your campaigns and likeability from your audience determines whether it was a hit or miss.

There is a gazillion of information available if you google around tracking productivity but, try a few before signing up with any of the best tools keeping in view of your data, security and price points. Remember that, you definitely need intelligent tools to map and track your productivity. Tracking everything in an excel sheet is not always a good idea.

"Hope is a weapon"

1. Defining Target Audience is quintessential and it takes trials to achieve
2. Hire experts, set up your target to track productivity
3. Rely on right tools to measure metrics
4. Run campaigns in tandem with all the areas of your company but not in silos
5. Measure your metrics periodically and adopt nimble strategies

Key Entrepreneurial Challenges for Start-ups during and Post Covid 19

Utkarsh Chaurasia

Hustling Student, Aspiring Entrepreneur

I am always a positive attitude person with a positive approach to everything and having effective problem solving skills. I always believe in fact, "Your thought process approach and the upbringing environment makes all the difference in you." I always work with a tentative plan and make it flexible to amend it according to futuristic conditions.

https://www.linkedin.com/in/petivirus
http://conference.nrjp.co.in/index.php/amds/article/view/497/480

Unexpected and unforeseen entry of a hailstorm when our business is climbing with a pace.

Moreover, this hailstorm is costing us so much. Talking of this Covid19 pandemic as this hailstorm, Covid19 has very high potential for the destruction of human resources. Numbers running with a high speed on a right upward inclination plane. Though this lockdown is getting to a huge economic loss for all countries, everyone is having prime priority as to save human resources. Economy lost can be recovered; lost human resources cannot be recovered.

"Every nation's economy is on a reboot, now, its role of entrepreneurial ecosystem and government support to recover and regain the growth...."

During this lockdown, everyone is feeling helpless for his or her venture, seeing live virus attack on his or her budget, say economy. Therefore, after lockdown, it is obvious that everyone focuses on loss recovery, but it should not be so. The loss is not for one, it is global and therefore, it is need of hour to join in hand and make the success of global recovery.

Entrepreneurs and managers have made changes in their approach to decision-making and leadership style. There is a need for unity and sympathetic decisions. Start-up ecosystem of any country has a marked impact on its economy, every nation will focus on this with backend support of existing industries, ventures and companies. The covid'19 pandemic making the impact on psychological, biological and economic factors to our life. Many mental health issues are arising these days and perhaps it is so obvious but we should not have been like this.For the next step guidelines for entrepreneurs, firms are coming up with their report on the same.

According to KPMG report, it's says,

"Business approaches during and after Lockdown Covid19:

1. Compassionate Leadership
2. Pragmatic yet agile business
3. Managing employee welfare

Managers and entrepreneurs must ensure that employees are maintaining physical distance but they should not be socially distanced means they should be socially connected and they have previous connection between them as a team.

Challenges after the economy reboot:

Lives vs livelihood
Everything we are doing to murder the virus is murdering the economy and this is the right sequence. However, no amount of CSR, government borrowing or printing money can substitute for the wages and self-employment income of our 50- crore labour force and their dependents. If the lockdown continues beyond two months, we must plan for citizens' well-being to move out of the commercial possibilities to the realm of fiscal policy.

Employers vs Employees
Employers cannot do deficit financing because they are rivers (flow) not oceans (stock). Shareholders and lenders do not pay salaries — customers do. It is a mistake to believe that Tata Steel, HDFC or Infosys are the typical Indian

employer — only 19,500 companies of our 6.3 crore enterprises have a paid-up capital greater than Rs 10 Crore.

Brilliant case in example : If schools do not receive fees, teachers are not paid.

Formal vs informal employment
Formal employment pays higher wages than informal employment because of the higher productivity that comes from access to talent, technology, and credit. However, the lockdown also demonstrates the higher resilience of formal employers to demand shocks, their ability to handle supply chain disruptions, and their efficacy as vehicles for traceable fiscal transfers.

Mind vs hand workers
The lockdown affects people who use their minds and hands differently — our guesstimate is that 65 per cent of our graduates can work from home but only 10 percent of our non-graduates can do so. In addition, while knowledge workers have delivered lockdown continuity from home, time will tell if they deliver productivity. Unscientific feedback about home working locked down employees suggests CEOs agree with Andrew Carnegie who answered the question "How many employees work at your company?" with "About half!"

Current vs the future generation
There is no doubt that governments should borrow massively to handle the crisis. However, the multi-decade narcissism of stealing from our grandchildren without a virus or world war has taken debt to 225 percent of global GDP and US student debt to $1.5 trillion (half of which was unserviceable before the crisis). Economic complexity and size allow higher advantage but this debt overhang blunts economic flexibility in handling the virus lockdown. Presentism is understandable in a crisis but trusteeship needs financial prudence.

Residents vs migrants
The virus will not change the reality of taking people to jobs rather than taking jobs to people, but it has exposed the ovarian lottery. The residents of West and South India have much lower vulnerability than the economic migrants from North and East India.The huge overseas diaspora of Kerala (about 10 per cent) and the huge Bihari diaspora in Kerala (about 9 per cent) expose how Kerala and

Bihar have been economic wastelands that forced migration for many of their residents.

Liquidity vs solvency

Employers fund themselves with debt and equity — equity is payable when able and debt is payable when due. The lockdown creates debt challenges and the RBI's recent measures were proactive, comprehensive and prudent. However, liquidity cannot solve solvency problems, central banks are not mandated to act as commercial banks and should be careful with "whatever it takes", and solvency problems need a fiscal response. European and American employers have been promised $8 trillion "virus" state loans and subsidies — about two years of their profits. India cannot afford this calibration but will need to do more.

Rule of written law vs law of spoken rule

The written regulatory cholesterol for Indian employers — 57,000 compliance, 3,100 filing and 4,000 annual changes — is painful enough without spoken rules like arresting employers for considering attendance in paying salaries, threatening employers for not providing housing, telling parents not to pay school fees, etc. Some of these are therapeutic or "fog of war" directives but they need discouraging in favour of a rule of law that is justiciable, documented and fair. Without employers, there are no employees.

These days every activity focuses on physical distancing and digital approach.

1. School and college teaching goes online
2. Supply chain merging with digitization
3. Digital bureaucracies will become mainstream: fast government decisions
4. Qualitative Growth over Quantitative
5. Boosting Employee's Morale
6. Opportunity in Adversity

Sha Alibhai

Director of Engineering

I'm a self taught software developer with almost 15 years experience. I'm passionate about using the lessons I've learnt to teach others how to maximize on their opportunities and grow to become the best version of themselves. Currently, I'm the Director of Engineering for an awesome company in the Medical Transportation space.

https://www.linkedin.com/in/sha-alibhai/

Let's start with a bold prediction.

Startups founded in 2020 are going to be disproportionately likely to be successful compared to those founded in previous years. There's a simple reason for this; determination. You have to be tremendously determined to start a company during a global pandemic, especially with talk of an impending recession. We've seen this pattern in the past.

Some of the largest companies in the last 20 years we're founded during the 2008 Great Recession - WhatsApp, Instagram, Slack and Uber just to name a few. When looking at what made these giants so successful, we can identify some clear common characteristics shared between them.

One is the determination to stick to a mission despite having to navigate a complex economic environment.

Another is to keep everyone rowing in the same direction, track outcomes and adjust course if necessary.

One of the most unique challenges presented to the business world in the midst of this pandemic has been the necessity to create a remote-first culture and establish processes that enable geographical distribution while still maintaining momentum and focus. In light of this, productivity tracking has become increasingly difficult, especially for those that habitually track outputs like the amount of invested hours in a particular pursuit over more outcome based impacts such as increased revenue. Luckily, enough lessons are being learned for us to start creating optimal strategies to amplify and track productivity in three key areas; people, process and innovation. Regular, surgical check ins at each departmental level that encourage open, honest discussion and clearly define next steps are vital in getting a constant pulse on an organization's health and put the accountability of solving the most immediate problems back on each individual.

My Favourite Quote:

A friend of mine, the founder of a company that grew to a billion dollars in annual revenue, best expressed the power of teamwork when he once told me, "If you could get all the people in an organization rowing in the same direction, you could dominate any industry, in any market, against any competition, at any time."
- The Five Dysfunctions of a Team, Patrick Lencioni

Synopsis in 5 Points:

1. Create an organization where everyone rows in the same direction
2. Start with the right goals
3. Focus on people, process & innovation
4. Follow processes that allow you to measure what matters, increase transparency and fail fast
5. Bring accountability back to each individual and show them how to identify and solve their most pressing issues

How To Emotionally Prepare To Launch a Startup During and Post Covid 19 ?

Srivats Grandhe
Founder

I am 52 years young and looking forward to establishing my startup i4Sight Technologies. I am working on setting up my start up since Jan 2020. Prior to this I was working with Eaton Towers as its Group Director - Operations Strategy for Africa region since 2015 based out of Kenya and UAE. Eaton Towers was acquired by American Towers in Dec 2019 and I decided to opt out of future employment to essentially chase my dream of starting up on my own. I am working on an opportunity that is yet to be addressed in the market and is an outcome of my experience and learnings during the last 19 years in the telecom sector across India, Africa & Middle East with Operators, OEMs and Tower Companies.

www.linkedin.com/in/srivatsgrandhe

I had just started off after registering my start up in UAE in mid March 2020 and was hit with the Covid lockdown. Hence I have been lucky this happened very early on with absolutely no impact to my plans. I have had to just reset my target dates according to the current situation.

Hence my emotional preparation didn't take a beating, it has given me time to sit back, explore my contact list and reach out to a few of them to bounce my thoughts off for a 2nd - Nth opinion on my startup idea. Our first approach for funding also got entangled in the

Covid related issues and was told it is going to be a while before they would come back to us for a discussion. I lost out on my co-founders as they were caught off guard with their own problems that were not anticipated.

Hence I am again exploring my circle of contacts to find like-minded individuals willing to explore and take the challenge to explore the opportunities in creating a platform that has no precedence as on date.

My famous quotes :

"Anything that won't sell, I don't want to invent. Its sale is proof of utility, and utility is success."
----- Edison

"We cannot solve our problems with the same thinking we used when we created them"
-----Einstein

Digital Marketing For Startup During & Post Covid-19

Tamara Toti
Founder

I am an avid storyteller who loves to bring brands to life through interactive and colourful content that has a positive impact on the community and world surrounding it.

https://www.linkedin.com/in/tamaratoti/

Digital marketing is essential for any business whether you are starting out or have been in business for a long time. The tools that come with digital marketing are valuable as they make it easier for people to find and connect with your business.

Nowadays, we are fortunate to have technology at our disposal, it has created and given us a boundaryless business life that makes the impossible possible.

Startups need to focus on strategies that speak to adaptability, regeneration, and renewal. When building and putting together a digital strategy you need to make sure you focus on how you are going to create a brand that stands out from the rest, that speaks to solving your clients problems and attract prospective clients in and after a crisis.

When Covid-19 hit all global economies came to a screeching halt, we saw some big businesses close their doors and popular publishing houses fell to their knees in the midst of this crisis because they had failed to create a strategy that spoke adaptability and never made the space in their strategies for change.

There must always be a contingency plan in place should the business not be able to come through the doors daily. Covid-19 has taught us that there is a new way to do business, businesses can reach out to their markets in many ways for instance Facebook and Instagram have come up with innovative ways that can be used to get their brands through crisis such as Covid-19, the possibilities are endless there are paid campaigns that cost next to nothing on Facebook or Instagram, podcasts and vlogs become an option and video events can all assist you with gaining traction.

It all starts with owning your business idea and driving it.

My advice is to make sure you know what brand voice you are using within your market, make sure you stay consistent to capture and keep a loyal following. Show your clients and prospective clients that you can be flexible, and no crisis can stop you from continuing the work that you set out to do.

Look at your competitors see what they are doing and try to create a strategy that displays your uniqueness but encapsulates the trends.

The great thing about digital strategies is that whether you are in the middle of Covid-19 or post Covid-19 the strategy can still be applied and used to open you up to new parts of the economy and market.

Most importantly, have fun with the process.

You make a living by what you get. You make life by what you give.
------Winston Churchill

Synopsis

1. Clear and consistent brand voice.
2. Create an adaptable digital strategy.
3. Use technology creatively and with set intention.
4. Put yourself out there
5. Have fun

How Can Seed Stage Startups Really Excel In Marketing In Tough Times

Building A Great Content Marketing Plan

Taher Dhanerawala
Entrepreneur

I am a co-founder of Rubberfy - A manufacturing startup with deals in manufacturing of household rubber products. Presently, my startup is in the stealth mode. A lot of brainstorming is going behind the scenes. I was born and brought up in Mumbai. I come from a middle class family. My father is a small time businessman. Taking his legacy forward, I am trying to achieve my mark in a startup world. I have done a bachelor in commerce from Mumbai University with the first class. Since then, I have done many odd jobs from selling newspapers to working in a BPO, so on and so forth. Till now, I had a roller coaster ride. I believe in self-learning. I choose skills over degrees. In my free time, I always look up for knowledge and upgrade my skills. I want to be a part of Indian startup ecosystem and contribute as much I can.

https://www.linkedin.com/in/taherd/

If you look up at an early stage startup, marketing plays an important role. I am a big fan of bootstrapping. Content marketing helps startups to target the right audience. It is important to make a content calendar well in advance.

A lot of people think that content marketing consists only in the form of writing, which is false. Content Marketing can be of any form, be it images, visuals, blogs, memes, etc. It is important for one's to find the right content marketing channel for their startups.

During a tough time like this, a startup can create a zero cost content marketing plan. You don't need to spend a single penny. Sounds strange right? Trust me it's very simple. I will lay down some essential steps which you can follow in your journey.

Make down the list of your targeted audience.

Once you do that it will be easier to follow the remaining steps. To begin with, use the relevant social media channels. You need to figure out where your target audience hangs. It doesn't mean you have to explore all the channels. Since social media is free to use, you can experiment with your content skills. Figure it out on various social media platforms.

LinkedIn is a great platform, to begin with.

You can find the leads easily. You don't need a social media manager for that. Try to spend at least an hour every day. Your efforts will not go in vain. The next platform which I like is twitter. Twitter is a great place to convey your marketing message in a few sentences in a creative way. You may end up hanging up with like-minded folks. If you have a good amount of Facebook friends, then it would be a great medium to market your content.

Remember, the FB ads are dead in my personal opinion. You may agree to disagree. However, google ad is also an option. But, I would recommend it to give it a try. Though it is competitive. You don't have to start with a big amount. Initially, you can bid a smaller amount and see how it works for you.

One important thing which you should keep in mind is never to use social bots to increase your followers. It will create a bad impact and will lead to bad engagement.

Never use robotic content tools. Remember, content marketing is a long term game. You won't get instant results. It takes time. It is as good as planting a seed. You need to be patient. 100 Genuine followers are better than 1000 fake followers. Initially, you can hire an intern to make a full-fledged content marketing plan for you. You may offer a basic stipend plus a learning growth for them. Your one brilliant creative with zero cost can make that viral. Tell your friends, relatives, and neighbors to support you. I am sure they will.

They will spread mouth publicity on your behalf. Remember the famous startup "Dropbox" how they started. They started with youtube marketing with their demo product, explaining about the features with the zero cost.

Remember that "Great Products do not need Marketing." Let people spread the word for you. Initially, you should focus on organic marketing rather than paid marketing. An organic way will help you in trial and error, and fix it without getting hurt.

You can use a free tool like Canva to create amazing ads. If you know someone from the influencer background who can help you with promoting your product without charging anything, and in return, you can offer him/her a product/service. Just like a barter system. These are some tricks you can apply during the initial stage of your startup.

These are some of the important metrics you should take care:

1. Follower growth
2. The number of time users spent on your site
3. Website traffic growth
4. Conversion Rate
5. Retention Rate

Track these metrics over a period of time. Analyse-it and see how it has worked for you. You will be overwhelmed to see the response. But, yes do not panic. Keep improvising until you get your desired result. Starting with Meme Marketing could be the best chance to attract the audience. Your creative appeal can make your product famous. Still, it's evolving, but as per my understanding, it's the best zero cost method to start with.

These are the key elements you can start by your own:

1. Keyword Research
2. Competitors Analysis
3. Buyers Personas

Make a content calendar according to these. Follow a strategy, and remember if it dont work, feel happy to change it. There is no rule book.

Good luck on your startup journey :)

"Don't worry about failure; you only have to be right once."
-- Drew Houston- Founder of Dropbox

Synopsis:

1. Content Marketing is a long term game. Play it wise.
2. Choose the channel which suits you, Experiment it, re-work it until it works.
3. You can start with zero budget. Yes, it works wonders :)
4. Hire an intern if required. Train him, guide him through the journey.
5. Last, but not the least - Engage with the audience, look at their pain points. Solve them and capture the market. Remember, customer satisfaction is the end goal.

How Can SaaS Startups Build Growth In Tough Times ?

Raj Swaminathan

Founder & Entrepreneur

A platform & solutions professional with over a decade-and-a-half of experience in building and scaling Adtech, Martech, B2B (SaaS/PaaS) businesses in India, Asia Pacific & Emerging Global Markets. Held senior management roles at some of the leading brands such as JWT, Genesis BCW, BharatMatrinmony.com, ValueFirst Digital and Mobusi. Consults leading global SaaS companies including Fraudscore.ai, Redtrack.io, Entent.io, Adverif.ai among others.

Founded and exited adtech startup AppDrive. Founder of StratumHub a consulting & advisory firm catering to global SaaS companies looking to enter India and APAC. Recently launched *'Wozzup With SaaS'* a community to keep updated on the SaaS ecosystem in India & Asia.

Avid traveller, a music aficionado and a home-chef

https://www.linkedin.com/in/itsraj/

"These are strange times" is a phrase that has been oft-repeated this year.

With the global economy sliding into recession due to the pandemic, businesses will change the way they operate forever. For many SaaS companies, this is probably the first time they will experience a recessionary climate in their existence with Salesforce.com and other early adopters of the SaaS model. The past decade has been kind and favorable to most SaaS companies that experienced a period of growth, as well as saturation as enterprises and businesses of all shapes and sizes, started to see the value in migrating from on-premise systems to the cloud. So how can SaaS companies survive this tough period and come out on top?

We look at five areas of focus, the **5 C's - Customer, Cashflow, Community, Capital & Change**

CUSTOMER

Customer Retention Is Priority

'Churn' will most likely hit all SaaS businesses forcing customers to pause the service or reduce costs. So in the short term, prepare for the downsell / downgrades and upsell when the market bounces back.

Relationships with essential stakeholder(s) within your customer's organization will be critical. Identify different stakeholders to mitigate the risk of over-dependence on one.

Strengthen current use cases and identify new use cases within existing customers. Seek out new use-cases with new customers. This applies in normal times but can be a differential in tough times. Increased usage of your application can result in stickiness to your platform.

Hyper communicate and personalize your outreach on your high-value customers (top 20%). Use smart automated communication and outreach for the rest (next 80%). Communicate everything ranging from offering help, taking feedback or sharing knowledge and content.

Bring In Efficiencies In Customer Acquisition:

Focus on revenue efficiencies despite the slow growth. Acquire profitable customers with shorter CAC periods and faster ROIs. In other words, focus on customers that generate cash. Deploy or scale alternate sales channels with lower acquisition costs, be it inside sales, inbound sales, or self-serve models.

Depending on your sales-model (top-down or bottom-up) you will need different kinds of attention in this phase. Top-down cases require alignment of your product or solutions with the strategic objectives of your customers. Whereas the bottom-up scenario would focus on increasing demand generation with more leads, demos, and trials. Identify and prepare as many potential customers that can convert eventually.

An obvious opportunity is to convert free users to paid users. These customers are already used to the product and can convert faster than new users. Focus on valuable and profitable customer segments and verticals with lower acquisition costs. Avoid high impact segments like travel etc.

Be empathetic to your prospects and communicate how your solutions can positively impact their business. Generic customer pitches might not cut ice, so make them specific, at least for high-value customers. Be a source of help and not a source of noise - add value beyond the deal.

CASHFLOW

If survival is key,then cash flow is the lifeline. Cash in the bank is the most important factor now. Therefore, aggressive efforts are needed to ensure actual collectible revenues and not just reaching sales closure data or vanity metrics. Taking a realistic outlook and considering the new costs of acquisition and current churn, the cash flow projections need reworking for the short or medium term.

Contextual cost-cutting is the need of the hour as opposed to a blanket approach. Optimize high fixed costs like office lease rentals, infra costs (servers / hosting etc). People are critical but reassess and plan cuts either cost-wise i.e salary cuts or headcount wise.

Manage accounts receivables efficiently. Regular communications with customer's stakeholders help build relationships and help assess customer's ability to pay and pay on time.

Restructure contracts for upfront payments and extended renewal periods. Don't give substantial discounts. It will make it difficult to revert to normal pricing later. Offer smaller discounts against upfront payment or long term contracts. Time-bound discounts that switch back to standard pricing within a few months.

COMMUNITY

Invest time and effort in building a community around your product or service. Having a forum or platform that your customers and users can rally around is a great way to build loyalty, retention and advocacy.

Content is a powerful way to cut through the noise if done right. Provide value keeping your target audience in mind. Focus on helping them solve problems related to their workflows or challenges they face in their role. Working remotely or moving their workloads from an office setting to home is a topic that is of keen interest. Content can also serve as a means to educate prospects who are furloughed or laid off to upskill themselves.

By giving them access to your SaaS platform as a tool to learn a new skill will help them advance their career and prove beneficial. By keeping them in focus SaaS businesses can nurture strong relationships that will convert into future customers.

Focus on platform and marketplace integrations that address challenges customers are facing in the current situation. This will make users more vested in your SaaS. Partner with complementary SaaS businesses to cross-sell your offerings. A horizontal SaaS can work well with a complementary vertical SaaS that is doing well or has higher demand.

CAPITAL

For all the SaaS startups that are seeking capital, debt should be more available to SaaS businesses compared to other verticals as the providers understand the value of recurring revenues. They may get conservative on the amount of money depending on the sign-ups and churn rates.

VC's continue to raise funds and remain open to investment opportunities in the SaaS space. The current situation provides investors with more leverage than founders. So SaaS founders need to tread with caution and have a clear vision for the investment.

So access to funds shouldn't be a challenge, but the right strategic match is what you might want to make sure.

CHANGE

The leadership needs to take up and drive change management. Remote working i.e Work From Home (WFH) is a big cultural change. The whole company needs to adapt and ensure work happens uninterrupted. The leadership should drive Teamwork, collaboration, and individual accountability top-down.

The confidence down the ranks that the business can run as usual despite the change is critical

This is a human crisis, over and above the business. This fundamental aspect needs careful handling with a lot of empathy and nuance. The drive, team spirit, and motivation should be maintained. It will reflect on the quality of work and hence goodwill in the long run with customers and prospects.

"Strength doesn't come from what you can do. It comes from overcoming the things you once thought you couldn't." Anonymous

Synopsis :

1. Retain existing customers on priority and stretch their engagement period.
2. Acquire new customers at lower costs & grab market share.
3. Cash in the bank is gold dust & meaningful cost cutting a must.
4. Invest in community, content & collaboration
5. Access to capital readily available but that musn't digress the pursuit for right investors
6. It is a human crisis above all so empathy, positivity & motivation helps collective resolve to tide over.

Global POV Summary

Bounce Back, Growth & Scaling Your Venture

Here is the synopsis of what has been shared by these experts, professionals and every learning awesome rockstars. Here are the pointers :

1. First focus on sustaining in tough times, profits can come later
2. Find new innovations & pivot fast
3. Have a clear & consistent brand voice
4. Believe in more organic marketing - Long term
5. Acquire new customers at lower costs but retain old customers at any cost
6. Invest more in community, content & collaboration
7. Pick up the right goals for your venture both short term and long term
8. There is an opportunity in adversity, Find some of them
9. Hire experts, set up your target to track productivity. They are the ones who can help you sail better. There is nothing like experience
10. Measure your metrics periodically and adopt nimble strategies to pivot fast
11. Use of AI will accelerate post COVID19
12. Industry 4.0 will see more innovative products and ideas going forward
13. Customer Experience strategy is the key to growth
14. **Pre-selling the new product idea even before a launch to ensure a right product market fit, validating pricing models, establishing customer partnerships will rise and become the next norm.**
15. The fundamentals of MVP during COVID-19 crisis include grasping the niche market before producing a multiservice provider, understanding and comprehending a valid consumer preference and value, choosing the proper platform for product launch, minimizing the cost of product development and using the best of resources via the MVP approach to save time and use it judiciously.
16. Effective utilization of technologies and forecasting your hiring needs well would certainly help you triumph
17. **Achieving and enhancing customer engagement in tough times is super critical**

18. Believe in Outcomation - It is more powerful : **Contribute directly to your** Business Goals and generate Impact through the adoption of its key drivers: Employee Engagement Index, Eliminating non-value Added processes, Robotic Process Automation, Insights Based Data
19. High CSAT score from existing customers, Time on Time
20. Post-Covid-19 brings the paradigm shift in translating science into workable solutions.

Here are 2 quotes that are about to change your life. Once you read them just shut down your eyes briefly and take a ride of imagination.

You will know what I am talking about.

You are the CEO
of your life.

@ravikikan

#RaviSupportMyStartup

RINSE REPEAT

Falling Is Not Failing
Failure Is Never Final

@ravikikan

#RaviSupportMyStartup

Understand These Quotes Like A Rockstar

Believe me & Trust me on this one.

Actually & Honestly, It is just not about business or growth or for that matter about bouncing back.

It is the right conditioning of your mind, body and your will to get things done in a positive frame of mind. I have done that time and again and I can vouch for this.

Why do I say that ? Well, I have failed more in life than I ever have had success , time and again. I have failed more miserably & went through depressive times that anyone could ever think of.

- I have had days when I had no money, everything lost in business
- I have had days when i was out of job and had no money or hope to get a new one
- I had my own share of ups and downs both in personal & professional life
- I had to struggle in my early days of my career so much that I hated this life
- I have struggled with weight, type 2 diabetes, high blood pressure
- I had struggled & failed miserably time and again, multiple times

One more thing that I understood in time was that the real thief of happiness for everyone is *"Comparison"* . This actually means that you would have to find your own definition of happiness and success and never compare it with anyone else as I shared before in my earlier chapters.

But what I always stuck on was the understanding that falling in not failing and failure in never final. I created my own opportunities in life and latched on to all hope and positivity. I worked on my strengths and ensured I learnt from my failures and moved ahead. Well I found my own set of happiness, joy and created my own small wins in life.

- I have been part of some awesome & successful startups that made money

- Have been working ever since with some successful & brilliant entrepreneurs
- I ran multiple half marathons and a full marathon after shedding obesity
- I have time & again mentored startups and have been a board advisor
- I had a good corporate career run at some of the leading brands
- I am still game for new challenges with God's grace

The sweetest and the most troublesome thing at the same time about starting or supporting a new idea or scaling your business is the fear and taste of the unknown. That's also the adrenaline rush if you understand.

However there is one caveat, when you are planning to jump in the whole abyss of a new idea , ensure you carry your parachute and your brains with you. Sometimes you would need things beyond your heart & feelings :)

Resilience and Patience. Rinse, Repeat.

A Little Prayer

Note To Self As Well

Now that you are all set, revise whatever notes you have made and the questions you have written. Try to answer all the questions you had noted with respect to your startup business idea.

This is going to be a long long journey for you and for your awesome dreams. Here is a small prayer for your journey that my mom always made me write on my books when I was a kid.

This has always been my Note To Self for new journeys in life, maybe this could be yours now going forward :

O God, O Lord,
To Thee I Pray,
Increase My Knowledge,
Day By Day.

May this prayer bring you a lot of hope, wellness and great success in life with leaps and bounds. I would also love to hear from you once you have read this book on your experiences and how you have dealt with the challenging times and how it has changed your own mindset.

Please feel free to share this book with anyone who might find it useful. That just might be your small contribution to the startup ecosystem ♥

Bon Voyage, My Friend :)

Best Wishes, Hugs & Hi5
Ravi Kikan

" You Don't Have To Be Great To Start But Have To Start To Be Great"
---- Zig Ziglar